Your Face Looks Familiar . . .

Your Face Looks Familiar . . .

How to Get Ahead as a Working Actor

Michael Bofshever

HEINEMANN
Portsmouth, NH

Heinemann
A division of Reed Elsevier Inc.
361 Hanover Street
Portsmouth, NH 03801–3912
www.heinemanndrama.com

Offices and agents throughout the world

Library of Congress Cataloging-in-Publication Data
Bofshever, Michael.
    Your face looks familiar . . . : how to get ahead as a working actor / Michael Bofshever.
        p. cm.
    Includes bibliographical references.
    ISBN 0-325-00763-2 (alk. paper)
    1. Acting—Vocational guidance. 2. Acting. I. Title.
    PN2055.B53 2006
    792.02'8'023—dc22   2005023155

Editor: Lisa A. Barnett
Production: Patricia Adams
Typesetter: TechBooks
Cover design: Night & Day Design
Manufacturing: Louise Richardson

Printed in the United States of America on acid-free paper

09 08 07 06 05 VP 1 2 3 4 5

This book is dedicated to the memory of my father,
Bernard Bofshever. Pleasant and Persistent.

Contents

Acknowledgments

Let me express my gratitude to all those who encouraged, enlightened, and promoted me along this journey. My good friend Allan Wasserman, who first suggested I write a book about actors. My sister Marilyn Brockway, who good-naturedly would ask, "Mike, when are you going to become famous?" Alexis Genya, who helped me start up my first acting class. Peter Funsten, who shared his soccer expertise and legal skills. Norman Hollyn introduced me to Bob Mecoy, who advanced the idea that I should create a seminar on the topic of how to make a life as a working actor. Todd Amorde with the Screen Actors Guild, who put me in contact with the executive director of the SAG Foundation, Marcia R. Smith. Bob Nuchow, Davidson Lloyd, and Jessie Bush from SAG, who promoted my seminars for the Life Raft Series. Screenwriter friend Sam Harper, who believed in the concept of my book and introduced me to writer Jon Winokur. Jon generously guided me through the early stages of this project with sound advice. Francis Solomita, who bolstered me as a writer. Confidant Peggy Flood counseled me with sage encouragement. Michael and Betty Howard, for their wisdom and lifelong friendship. Lynn Masters, for her Speech and Voice classes. The sound judgment of Paul Salzman and the Guidance Center. Laura Fogelman, for lovingly representing me at Independent Artists Agency. Richard Marion and our conversations at the Farmers Market. Jim Muldoon's friendship,

Jerome Lutnick's encouragement, and Larry Singer's professional support. Director, producers Mark Rydell and Tommy Lynch, for believing in my acting ability. Friends Marybeth Raymond, Michael Weinglass, and Betsy Robinson, for marketing promotions and insights. Web designer John Snyder's creativity. Production editor Patty Adams and copy editor Beth Tripp's comprehensive work. Leslie Allan-Rice, for optimistically and tenaciously managing my career. All the actors who have inspired me with their artistry and commitment. My editor, Lisa A. Barnett, whose sound judgment and humor nurtured me through this process. My beautiful wife, Celia Lee, and our pride and joy, our daughters, Jessica and Katie, I love you.

Introduction

Many years ago when I was about to graduate from the theater school at Boston University, I was cast in a production of *Richard III* for the Theater Company of Boston, starring Al Pacino. The cast were primarily working New York actors, plus a few college students like myself. The first *Godfather* film had just been released and the fact that I was acting in a play with Al Pacino had my head spinning. Rehearsals were in a warehouse space in downtown Boston. During rehearsal we had a problem solving a scene that I was acting in. Al volunteered to direct me and the other two actors. Now I was not only acting with Al Pacino but was also being directed by him. The production was at Harvard University's Loeb Theater. Whenever Al was in the green room before the show, I would make my way there so I might listen to him talking with fellow cast members. I loved listening to his stories of working with Marlon Brando. Here's one that I never forgot: Al was watching Brando struggling to put on a pair of slacks. Al asked him why he was getting dressed in such an odd manner. Brando replied, "Don't you get bored doing the same routine over and over again? I thought I would try getting dressed using one hand to see what that was like." The consummate actor, continuing to explore—how perfect. One day before a performance, Al came into my dressing room and asked me for a favor. "Mike, when you enter as the First Murderer," he said, "would you mind making a sound so as to motivate my turn towards you?" I lit up. My heart pounded faster. I said, "Sure Al, not a problem." I remember I could hardly say his name out loud. The production ran for two months and was my first venture into the professional world. The point of this production was to be able to explore the material without the pressure of reviews. Al later went on to make an award-winning film about this exploration, titled *Looking for Richard*. Here I was about to graduate college, with the opportunity to act in this production and thinking, Boy, have I got it made! With a the-ater degree, a season of summer stock under my belt at the Tufts Arena Theater, where I made a whopping twenty-five dollars a week, and a pro-fessional acting credit, I was sure I was on my way to fame and fortune. College had not at all prepared me for the harsh realities of pursuing a professional career as an actor, however. Little did I know how little I knew!

Upon graduation I returned home to Brooklyn, New York, not sure what I was going to do next. I found an apartment in Queens and lived there for a year with my girlfriend while working as a groundskeeper at the Westside Tennis Club. I began taking acting classes in New York City with the legendary acting teacher Michael Howard. When my girlfriend and I broke up, I crashed on a buddy's couch on the Upper West Side for several months until I found a fifth-floor walk-up studio apartment in Chelsea. I took odd jobs to support myself. I worked as a waiter, a furniture mover, a building superintendent, a house painter, and eventually a bartender in Greenwich Village. My youth, coupled with an abundance of enthusiasm, overcame my fears and my ignorance of how to earn a living as an actor. However, I quickly realized that no matter how much I fantasized other-wise, stardom was not in the cards for me. I continued studying acting with Michael Howard, developing my craft and learning how to access my inner life, which was a very frightening process. My instrument was so filled with rage. I was holding on to a deep-seated hurt that I did not know what to do with. With his encouragement, I began to tap into that well of emotion and use it in my work with great success. Accepting what was going on with me, and merging it with the character I was working on in a scene, enabled me to grow as an artist and as a person.

Frustrated by my lack of progress in finding acting work and unsure of what I wanted to do, I dropped out of acting class and fell in love with the life of being a bartender in the Village. During this period I took on a job as a stage manager at the famed Actors Studio. It afforded me the opportunity to watch acting classes and act in some Studio projects (I was in the original workshop production of *The Best Little Whorehouse in Texas*). Having an opportunity to watch Lee Strassberg conduct acting classes and see famous members such as Ellen Burstyn, Harvey Keitel, and Al Pacino sit in and comment on actors' work was inspiring. It helped me realize how much I wanted to act—not become a star, just act.

I remember one night at the restaurant where I worked when a regular plopped down on his favorite bar stool near closing time. He was well into his fourth or fifth cocktail of the evening and he began to bemoan his lost direction in life. If only he had hung in there and kept after his dream and had not gotten carried away with all the sensual pleasures and drunken nights. It was a moment of truth for me. You can imagine it in a film. The customer sitting at the bar just before closing time, crying in his drink. The appropriate sad song pours from the jukebox and fills the smokey room. The director slowly moves the camera lens onto a close-up of the young bartender's face. In his face you can see the recognition that this could be him if he doesn't make a commitment. Walking home at two in the morning, I realized I hadn't truly invested myself in becoming an actor. I was just testing the water, sticking my toe into the ocean, when what I needed to do was dive in fully. I did not want to live with the regret of not trying hard enough.

I returned to Michael Howard's acting class with a vengeance. I worked on challenging scenes and exercises to help me grow as an artist. I read the trade papers and auditioned for anything I felt I was right for. I waited endlessly on line at Equity open calls. I did extra work in commercials, acted in industrial films, and did under-fives (roles with five lines or fewer) in soap operas. I made the rounds, dropping off my 8 by 10, looking for an agent. I became a founding member of a theater company. Whenever things didn't go my way, which was often in the beginning, I would tighten my belt, deal with the loss, and become more determined never to quit.

I have been a working actor now for more than thirty years. I've had the good fortune to have been a series regular and I've made countless guest-star appearances on episodic television. I have been featured in fifteen motion pictures and acted in several hundred television commercials. As an actor-director-producer of an acting company, the Actors

Producing Company, I was involved in developing new plays for seven years in New York City with my colleagues. I have acted on stage in Los Angeles, Off Broadway in New York, in summer stock, and in regional theaters. As a director I have been part of the creative process of directing new plays on both coasts. I became a director member of the Playwright/Director Unit of the Actors Studio in Hollywood. My love of the craft of acting and my ability to convey this knowledge helped me become a well-respected acting teacher.

An actor cannot rely on talent alone. He must also be industrious, creative, hopeful, and persistent. An acting career has no guarantees. Perseverance is key, but there are many who do not get the breaks needed to enable them to earn a living as an actor. The road to success has no limits, no final destination, no singular way to get there. The statistics supplied by the acting unions suggest that the odds are overwhelmingly against you earning a steady living as a performer. Yet so many of us are willing to chance all that. We believe in our heart of hearts that, given the opportunity, cast in that one role, we have something to offer. That we can make a difference and be recognized for our work.

We go on pursuing our elusive dream. The nobility lies in taking action with determination and hopefulness. I have had the good fortune to have earned my living doing what I always wanted to do. My wife and I have raised a family and sent our children to college. At times I've earned a steady income from residuals for film, television guest-star appearances, and commercials, while other times we have had to scramble to pay the rent. To succeed as an actor is to be a survivor. My intention is to show how my acting colleagues have made their journeys, to share our knowledge with those beginning or those who may have gotten lost on the way. I want to attest that in between the celebrity artist whose name and face are instantly recognizable and the unknown struggling artist, there is a contingency of rank-and-file actors who show up, do their job, and live the life of a working actor.

At first I interviewed several acting friends of mine on audiotape. I asked them to tell from their experiences what their life as a working actor is like. I wanted to know how they managed to persevere, how they dealt with the numerous obstacles they faced, and what tools they used to succeed. One actor would then recommend another to me. It became *Six Degrees of Separation*. As my interviewing skills improved, I was able to recognize something in the voice or a sparkle in the eyes that was unique to that individual. I then transcribed the recordings, with minor editorial changes. The actors who participated thoroughly enjoyed reminiscing and sharing the vast knowledge they have gained along the way. If you are interested in learning more about a particular artist, I encourage you to go to the Internet and search for a more definitive biography.

While I was doing my research, a former acting student of mine, Todd Amorde, introduced me to Marcia R. Smith, the executive director of the Screen Actors Guild Foundation. I told her that I was interested in moderating a panel discussion on the journey of the working actor and that I was prepared to discuss what it takes to create and maintain a career as an actor. Marcia felt that, with my credentials as both a working actor and a teacher, I could offer something that would be useful to the SAG membership, and she gave the project a green light under the auspices of the SAG Foundation Life Raft Series. The James Cagney Room at the headquarters of the Screen Actors Guild in Los Angeles was packed with fellow actors. With a panel of four experienced actors, I led a discussion on how to succeed in show business. I sensed in the room an unquenchable thirst for the knowledge my panelists and I wanted to share. At the close of the evening the actors and I were surrounded by our colleagues, still wanting to know more. It was one of the most rewarding experiences I have ever been associated with. I have made this a recurring event in Los Angeles and New York because of the overwhelmingly positive response and the SAG Foundation's encouragement.

Many of the actors in this book have at one time or another been approached by someone with a quizzical look on his face. It is almost as if we have made some personal connection. We're aware that perhaps you may have seen our work on stage, on television, or in a film. It feels good to be recognized, since we are not inundated as celebrities often are. We are frequently asked, "Your face looks familiar; do I know you?"

"Yes," I reply with a warm smile, "I'm a working actor."

Michael Bofshever
Santa Monica, California
www.michaelbofshever.com

Your Face Looks Familiar . . .

CHAPTER ONE

So You Want to Be an Actor?

Whenever I moderate a Journey of the Working Actor panel discussion for the SAG Foundation Life Raft Series, or when I speak with college students at university theater departments throughout the country and most recently at the American Film Institute (AFI), I begin with what I consider to be the cornerstone of building a successful acting career. The common thread that all working actors possess is a deep, committed passion for the work. This intense, emotional craving to act is what drives an actor forward. Without this desire, why else would you put yourself through all the struggles that are necessary to succeed as an actor? There are countless other ways to earn a living and still have a rewarding life. An actor's passion is a treasure chest of emotions that fuels an actor's creativity. This reminds you of why you need to be an actor when confronted by the numerous challenges that will be in front of you. You draw upon your passion as a living, breathing life force of energy. Actors with passion have a responsibility and a desire to share their gift with audiences in order to feel fulfilled as an artist. Each actor discovers this passion at different times in his life. When it eventually takes hold on your soul, you'll be smitten with the acting bug and you will do virtually anything to satisfy this creative craving.

I started every interview for this book by asking the actor to recall his or her earliest memories of when he or she first was introduced to acting. Was it a specific incident or an accumulation of experiences that eventually drew that individual into dreaming of one day becoming an actor? For anyone who is on this path and is seeking affirmation, it is important to know that there is no one type of person that becomes a performer. The actors interviewed for this book come from all over the United States and some from as far as Australia and India. Their economic backgrounds are as varied as the populations they represent. No one had the advantage of growing up in an established show-business family nor had connections that made it easier for him or her to get started. Everyone I interviewed started from square one and managed to work his or her way up the ladder of success. Some actors had a parent who acted in community theater. Several parents of these actors instilled in their children the importance of going to live theater as a cultural adventure for the family. Seeing a play for the first time as a child connected these future performers to the magic of the event. Some identified with the characters on stage as they acted out their problems in front of the audience. Intuitively they became hooked by the dramatic conflict of the play and its endless problem-solving possibilities.

There is also no single personality trait that is a prerequisite to becoming an actor. For some who were terribly shy, acting became a way to express themselves in a way they previously could not. For others, who had a more outgoing persona, the adulation from approving audiences was an ego boost. Some people found acting a way to release pent-up feelings. Dancers looked for greater expression through acting because of injury or a need to explore different creative avenues. Class clowns who enjoyed making others laugh went on to improvisation classes and channeled their misbehaving into a useful tool as an actor.

Since there is no time limit to when someone can become bitten by the acting bug, some people may discover their love of acting as an adult. For several semesters I taught acting at UCLA Extension. It was a program for adult nonprofessionals to further their education. These people came from all walks of life, and many of them fell in love with acting because it afforded them the possibility to be playful and childlike in their grown-up world. Several senior citizen students went on to study with me in my professional class. They were excited to open another chapter in their lives.

As you become a more seasoned actor, who over time must face the harsh realities of the profession, it is important to remember why you wanted to act in the first place. It comes from your passion. The joy you initially experienced from playing pretend. The exaltation that comes with expressing yourself and affecting others. You will be able to draw upon this foundation when tested, as the basis of your need to act. Never lose sight of what brought you to this journey. If you believe this is your *calling* and remain true to its roots, it will give you the strength to continue to lead a creative life.

Debra Monk: I went to college late—I didn't have enough money to go to college, and that college said it would pay for your tuition if you [said] you would be a teacher. One of the courses you had to take was speech class. It was a very small college. The guy who taught the speech class was also the director of the theater. I did a couple of speeches and he said I should try out for his play. I said, "I've never seen a play," which was true. I tried out for it and I got it. It was the *Birthday Party* [Harold Pinter]. I was totally green. I didn't know anything. When he said, "Let's run it"— I didn't know any terms—"blocking"—I had no idea. Nobody [had] met anybody like me in that department. Then I fell in love with it. I had never seen anybody happy at their work. I didn't know that existed. When I discovered people did this, I asked, "Do people do this for a living? I'm going to do this, this is really fun." I became totally passionate about it.

Armin Shimerman: I had just transferred from New Jersey to Santa Monica and had no friends whatsoever. My mother thought it would be good if I met people. We met a distant relative who was teaching an acting class at the Jewish Community Center; [my mother] suggested that I should take his class. Which I did. In high school the teacher was looking for an actor to play John Proctor in *The Crucible*. No one knew me there because I was a relatively new student in high school. The teacher took a chance on me and cast me as the lead. I felt I found something that I could do. I felt good about doing it. People were complimentary about it. And I was making friends at the same time. But more importantly it just seemed like the perfect fit. On rare occasions I would be transported. That is why I continued to do it, never thinking it was really going to be a career. It only morphed into a career when everything I did was successful.

Vic Polizos: It was my whole persona, really, when I was young. The church thought I was the designated young actor and speaker. When there was the church's twenty-fifth anniversary celebration for the governor, [out of] everybody of Alabama, I was chosen to speak—to narrate the proceedings—and I was only eleven, twelve years old. Whenever there was a Greek play, I was the guy who got to do the lead. It was what brought me recognition. It was the only thing. I was a pretty chubby little Greek kid who made decent grades but certainly was restricted to what he could do because of his parents. This was the only place I could fly and it became *mine*. I got attention and people praised me for it, and it was such a great feeling.

Magda Harout: My history was kind of made for me. I was born into an acting family. My parents, my mother, father, grandfather, grandmother, aunt, two uncles were all actors. They were all born in Armenia or Russia. My grandfather had his own acting company called the Antranik Dramatic Company. They were considered the Armenian Barrymores. The whole family were actors. That's how they got out after the [Russian] Revolution. They went on tour and never came back. [*laughs*] They sold everything, went on tour all through Europe, ended up in the Middle East, [then] down towards Italy, up to France, London, New York. Wherever there was an Armenian community, they put on a play. I was born in Detroit. We ended up in California, which was their goal—they wanted to be in movies. My dad started a restaurant business on Ivar. After a few years he was established. They were working with old movie stars that nobody knows about. He built a theatre, the Ivar Theatre, right on Ivar. Then he moved up on the [Sunset] Strip and it became a hangout for actors and so on. I was brought up in that milieu. I was named after a play. My mother was pregnant. They were doing a German play by Suderman called *Magda*, and they named me after that character. So I was kind of brought up that way. Other kids were out playing and I was under the table, listening to rehearsals.

Rif Hutton: I was always performing in some manner or fashion as far back as I can remember. I'm an air force brat. I was the runt of a brood of six kids. My brothers, when they were the new kids in town, would fight all their classmates. Me being the runt, that wasn't a possibility, so I had to entertain my way—that was my way of socializing. I was a little bit of a talkative troublemaker in class. The New Jersey Symphony boys chorus came around. I was in Catholic school; they came around auditioning at the schools. The nuns insisted as part of my punishment for something I had done that I audition. That was the first—I was actually getting paid to perform. After I got over the initial stage fright, I just fell in love with that. Military kids—we didn't have a lot of money—big family—so to be able to come home and flash an extra twenty bucks in front of my big brothers was pretty cool.

Sheila Kelley: What drew me to want to be an actor was probably my inability to communicate on my own, with my own words as a person in the world. I was very shy and I had an enormous amount of emotional life going on. I couldn't communicate well because of that shyness. The acting gave me characters and words and ways of funneling out all this incredible emotional life inside of me to the world. I could communicate with the world better. It was a means of communication for me. That's what drew me to it, that's why I started doing it.

Julio Oscar Mechoso: I used to do impressions. I was always the class clown. In sixth grade my nickname was *Problema*. The principal, the PE teachers said, "There goes Problema." I was always the class clown. In junior high I started imitating people, different actors. I came from a tough little neighborhood, where being an actor wasn't really a thing you wanted to brag about. There wasn't much opportunity there or reinforcement from my peer group or my environment. Finally when I went to high school, I said, "Why not?" [and I took an acting class]. For the first seven or eight months I was very shy and trembled a lot and got very nervous. One day I took off with a character and that was the first time it bit me.

Lauren Tom: I started out as a dancer—I started a bit late to train as a dancer. I think I was fourteen when I started taking lessons. I just fell in love with it because I was a bit shy at the time. Dancing felt like the perfect expression because you didn't have to talk. I'm from Highland Park, Illinois, so I was dancing in a dance company there [Lou Conte Hubbard School Dance Company]. The show *A Chorus Line* came through town, the first national tour. There was a part in there for a short Asian girl. I think they didn't have a lot to pick from at that time. My friends dragged me to the audition because I didn't sing or act but I could dance really well. I auditioned and they took me [*laughs*], so it was kind of mindblowing. I was seventeen and they had to wait until I turned eighteen, so I didn't have to have a guardian come with me. They trained me on the road. They gave me acting lessons and singing lessons. I still remember that I was so shy and so terrified that every time when my character had to take a few steps forward to do my story—every time I'd say a line—I'd take a step back, till I was back in the line with everyone else. The people who were to the left and right of me would push me forward because I didn't realize I was doing that.

Andrew Prine: I first got the acting bug really and truly in one evening in Jacksonville, Florida. I was staying with my mother and then-stepfather—I was thirteen years old—they took me to my first professional play. I had never seen a play. It was in a tent—a traveling show—they were doing *Showboat*. I looked at these beautiful people running down the aisles of the tent and getting on stage in the center under the lights. It was magic. I realized right then that I was an actor. It struck me like a bolt of lightning. I walked out of the tent afterward with my mother and stepfather and said, "I'm an actor." My mother said, "God help us. The boy is in the fifth grade and he cannot read and he's an actor." I said, "That's it, I'm an actor." From then on I knew that was it. Everything was going to be pointed towards that, though I knew really nothing about it at all. Everything in high school was directed secretly or overtly toward acting. I hated school, I wasn't very good in school, but I was completely obsessed with the idea of acting.

Klea Scott: I was born in Panama, raised in Canada. Came to the United States when I was nineteen, to New York City. My earliest recollection of acting was probably Judy Garland's performance in *The Wizard of Oz*. It was the reason why I decided to become an actor. I must have been five or six when it struck me. It actually led me to beg my mother for tap dance lessons. I just adored the film; it moved me so much. Dance lessons was really the crux of the backyard show. Me and my sisters were the lords of my neighborhood. We put on shows all of the time. We had programs. I remember the big show and I was always bossing everyone around. Choreographing everything—putting myself in the center of everything—it was very song-and-dance. I then had this strange luck in Ottawa, Canada, to be on a children's television show [*You Can't Do That on Television*] when I was about eleven years old.

Stephen Mendillo: I saw a play once when I was young. I went to the theater—my mother took me. I think it was . . . *Long Day's Journey into Night*. I saw people wrestling with their problems. It was so great to see people hacking it out up there. Dealing with things. And you get to sit there and watch and you think, "Yes, yes, I recognize that." They're into the battle; they're actually discovering it. It's out in the open. People are confronting each other. And you're learning something about this. That was the moment that I thought this is really worthwhile. Then I thought for me, my personality, my education, sort of how I am. I figured I'm a physical person, but I'm also an intellectual person. I'm not a well-disciplined person. So therefore I'm not a good writer. I don't sit down and do the good, hard, quiet work of writing. Acting is collaborative. I always liked this about actors. I also have felt the playwrights have said things that are on my mind better than I could. So what better way to bring ideas, badly needed ideas, to the world, the people of the world, than to be an actor.

Nike Doukas: I've always liked to perform. I can tell you every single play that I was in since kindergarten on. I love storytelling, and my parents were serious theater-goers. I think I really like the attention. I loved the storytelling aspect of it, the make-believe part of it, but I really liked the attention. I was the youngest of four and everybody in the family had a really strong personality and you had to work really hard to be heard. I loved the feeling of being on stage and everyone had to be quiet and listen to me. It was kind of a creative way of getting that attention. I also came from a really creative family that really valued the arts, so I saw it as something important. Mostly I liked the showing off. Even when people say, "I don't know how can you get up in front of people," that is not something I even think about. That's the part that is easy. I like being the center of attention when I'm on stage. There is nothing better than being on a dark stage with the light on you. That feels safe to me.

John P. Connolly: My mother dabbled as an actress when she was in high school. One summer—I think I was fourteen years old—I was driving her crazy, as were my brothers and all my friends. She grabbed me and my best friend and threw us into the car and drove us over to the Catholic church, our local parish. She told me, "Get out! Get out of the car and don't come back until this activity is over!" I said, "Ma, what are you doing? You can't just take us away and make us do things." She said, "Yes I can—I can't stand you, get out of the house." She drives away. Me and my best friend, Michael, are standing there and we looked down into the church basement and all we saw were girls. There were girls everywhere. We thought, whatever the hell it is, it ain't half bad if it's all girls. So we went down there and found it was the summer Catholic Youth Organization Theater [program]. They were doing *Bye Bye Birdie*. We got involved in that as a summer activity. Kept us out of the house, kept us out of my mother's hair, and we had fun and met all these girls. It was a lark.

Juanita Jennings: I was inspired as a little girl—my mom and I would go to the movies once a week—I went to see a movie called *Imitation of Life* with a black actress named Juanita Moore. I was so blown away by the production—I could feel what was going on. I had never seen up to that point a black woman or a man [portrayed] with such dignity. She was doing a different style of acting for that time; it was very honest, very today. She just blew me away. It was such an emotional piece, I got pricked there. I knew from that point on I wanted to do this.

Hal Landon: My parents were actors. My dad in the 1940s did a few films, mostly war films and Westerns. He was in [*It's*] *a Wonderful Life*, had a part in that. He did a lot of community theater work, which I went and saw. He was a good actor and my mother was also very good. She never did it professionally, but she also worked in the community theater. I was exposed to that, but I think I took it for granted. It wasn't a big thing to me. I never had acting aspirations. I knew I could do it, but I wanted to play in the NFL or the NBA. When the harsh reality of too short, too slow hit me—I was a sophomore in college—I was looking for something to do, so I took an acting class. Then I did a small part in a community theater and I got a big response from it. That was when I said, "I want to do this." Before I got out of college I made this shift; what I really wanted—I didn't want to be a star—was to work in theater. That was the direction I wanted to go.

Clyde Kusatsu: I was born and raised in Honolulu, Hawaii, fourth-generation Japanese American. Back when I was a kid we had only one [TV] station. I was one of those weird kids that didn't care to go out on the sand at the beach. Inside I always felt there has got to be more than this, even though it's considered paradise. In a sense I grew up with all the Mickey Rooney, Judy Garland [movies], "Hey, let's make a play." We used to do talent shows. I was in the choir—I liked singing—of an all-boys Episcopal school when I was fourteen. The choir teacher said to me, "Would you like to be in the chorus of *Guys and Dolls*?" I did and—boom!—it was a new world. We were in an all-boys school and there were girls in there and we were making a play, doing a musical. All this makeup, and it was like, wow! I really felt like I fit in. I couldn't fit in on the athletic field, but give me a dance routine, I could do that.

Erick Avari: My dad owned movie theaters in India—we called them cinema halls—and I was fascinated with movies. We'd go to the movies and I would make my mom tell me the stories again on the walk home just so I could relive the experience. That was clearly where I got the fascination for the whole genre. Then I met a director when I was nine years old, a Bengali director, Satyajit Ray. He was over at our house for tea. There was something that was really fascinating about him, the way he spoke, the way he conducted himself. I asked him, "Uncle" [everyone in India is uncle], "what do you do?" He said, "I make pictures." I asked him, "How do you do that?" He said, "Would you like to come see?" He would send a Jeep for me after school; [I would] drive down to the set and I would hang out with him for a couple of hours every day for the next three weeks. There was something that was so fascinating about everything that was going on. That was when it really jelled in my head that I wanted to be an actor.

Amy Hill: I didn't see people like me in movies or television, so this was something of a private dream of mine. I remember the first year of high school, looking at the possibility of drama class and thinking it was too scary. Somehow I felt that if I signed up, people would look at me and say, "What are you doing here?" I didn't sign up that first year. Even though I was in a school that was multiracial, with a lot of African Americans, Asians, I still felt I was not allowed to be in that special place. For some reason I got up the courage to sign up for drama class and the first acting exercise—you had to sit in a chair and go from being a baby to a really old person—I did it. The teacher thought I was brilliant. Who knows what he was thinking, but he was really, really supportive of me. That one teacher shifted my whole perspective of . . . what was possible.

Anne-Marie Johnson: I picked up on the gangly, comedienne aspect of Lucille Ball. At that age [five years old] I was exceptionally tall and thin. I just felt a relationship with the physicality and the humor and I knew that I had that in me. I was always a very extroverted child, very friendly and outgoing. I just felt a calling. It was very odd. I was very comforted by the images and knew that was what I wanted to do even though I knew nothing about it. My parents supported it. It was a calling; it wasn't a spiritual calling, I think it was a physical calling. [*laughs*] I felt that was what my body, my being could do.

Aaron Lustig: Girls. That was the motivating thing that got me into acting. That's actually true. I wasn't the most popular kid there in eighth grade. I got the lead in *Bye Bye Birdie*. I got to play Conrad Birdie. Which for a short, bald, Jewish guy—I wasn't bald in eighth grade, but you could see it coming even then. [*laughs*] It helped with my popularity. When I was on stage I felt important. The girls' screaming helped. That was really the first reason I wanted to do it. Of course the bug hit instantly and I loved acting from the very get-go.

CHAPTER TWO

Ready, Set, Go!

As you embark on this journey—your career—take a moment to ask yourself this vital question: In your heart of hearts, is there anything else in the world that you feel you can do with your life that would provide you with as much fulfillment as acting does? If your answer is no and you truly believe that you have the passion, talent, and fierce determination to succeed, then you are ready to get started on this adventure. From my own experiences and those shared by the actors interviewed in this book, I can tell you there is no one formula on how to succeed in this business. Some actors get a lucky break early in their career, thanks to their looks or talent. They might have great success for a limited time, only to fade away as the years go by. Other actors struggle for a long time trying to get started, yet slowly they are able to build a reputation as a competent, capable working artist. Only a very few actors attain outright fame and are able to remain at that level for their entire career. The vast majority of working actors don't go into the profession with such high expectations. Rather, we strive to live up to those two words: *working actor*. Let me dispel the myth that an actor has to attend a prestigious university and major in acting to become successful. Certainly, the best-known university programs that offer "showcase" productions upon graduation in New York and Los Angeles offer a leg up for their students to meet with casting directors and talent agents. Acting in college will give you the basics of the craft of acting, and a cadre of friends to begin to network with, but it will not guarantee you work in the professional world. Most young actors will need to continue their training with a challenging and trusted professional acting teacher. You must recognize that while the business is always looking for fresh new faces, there are still more experienced actors who have put in their time before you with professional credits on their resume. Many well-known or industry-recognizable actors never attended college or even studied acting until they discovered a professional acting program in Los Angeles or New York. However, it *is* essential to have a college degree so that you have something to fall back on, should you decide to move on to another profession.

Once you have made the commitment to either New York or Los Angeles, first and foremost you need to find a place to live and employment to support yourself. Whatever type of survival job you find, make sure it is flexible enough for you to go to auditions. Opportunities in the beginning may be few and far between, and you don't want to miss out on a single audition. It is also important when first starting out to continue to invest in yourself. Paying for acting class may mean you may have to take on a second or third job. You may need to forego certain material pleasures in order to take a needed voice or dance lesson. If you put the time in now, it will continue to pay dividends in the future. During this time you will need to focus on the larger picture when things are not happening as quickly as you would like them to. Patience is a virtue. When a colleague signs with an agent or gets an acting job, it can become discouraging when you have worked just as hard and haven't gotten that break yet. You want to know when it will be your turn. A good friend should be supportive of a peer's success. When the time comes and you're the one who's gotten the lucky break, remember to be helpful in whatever way possible. When I was first starting out as a young actor in New York, my acting friends and I would hold a space for each other at an open Equity call, recommend each other for work, and share information about casting opportunities. Most importantly, be there for your colleagues when they need encouragement. Remind them how talented they are and encourage them to hang in there. Many of my closest friends today are the ones that I began my career with in my fledgling days in New York. It is remarkable when you are young and ambitious how far your hopes and dreams can take you with so little money in your pocket.

When I hold seminars on the journey of the working actor, I emphasize the importance of creating your own work. Actors want to know how they can get an agent or why they aren't getting cast when they're auditioning so well. Waiting by the phone is a maddening way to live. Praying you will be discovered while sitting in your room is a waste of time. So much of this business is out of your control, but the one thing you can do is develop a project for yourself to act in. That means you need to belong to, or start up, a company of like-minded individuals that wants to produce plays. When I was starting out, several of my acting friends and I started up a theater company. We invested our own money to produce two plays that summer. We did all the work, from building sets and creating costumes to working the box office. It had that "let's turn that barn into a theater" quality that I fondly look back on. In seemingly a short amount of time, we had actors asking us for work, directors looking to be interviewed, and playwrights submitting plays for the company to produce. Agents and casting directors came to see our company perform. By being actively involved, an actor places himself out in front. You can also raise your visibility by expanding your creative boundaries and writing a piece you can perform. Actors who naturally have an ear for dialogue and character development may become some of the best writers. By producing, creating, or writing your own work, you are taking charge of your career. Your job is to act! When you do so, good things will happen.

A major issue for any actor is landing an agent. It is a classic Catch-22: you need work to get an agent; you can't find work without an agent. You finally land work but you can't get an agent to see you. You pound the pavement, submit your headshot and résumé, and still no agent. You feel like you are beating your head on the wall with no end in sight. Since we are not going to pattern our professional life on the exception—the actor who gets signed right out of college—how do we get signed with an agent? You must realize before you enter an agent's office that she has an established client list of actors she is working with. For her to be interested in you, she has to believe that when you audition you will get work and represent the agency in a positive way. The agent is looking to make her 10 percent based on your talent and looks. So what can you do to make yourself more attractive to a potential agent? You need to be acting in something so he can determine if it is possible for him to add you to his client base. It is therefore your responsibility to be acting, so as to be seen. That means if you are not getting cast by an established theater company, you must—I dare to repeat myself—create your own work to be noticed. Here's another possible scenario: You are acting in a production and have been unable to get someone to come down and see you. Lo and behold, another cast member has an agent who comes to see her work, and voilà, the agent discovers you. This has happened to me twice. Agents and managers came to see their clients and asked me to sign because they liked what they saw when I was performing. Every actor faces this fortunate dilemma once in a while. Good things will happen for you, sometimes when you least expect it, if you are out there doing your job.

All actors at one time or another have done mailings of their picture and résumé to agents with the hope of getting noticed. They spend hours submitting themselves. I have never heard of this as an effective way to meet an agent. Yes, there will be exceptions; a beautiful person, for instance, may be noticed, but for the most part it gives you a false sense of accomplishment. What I would suggest—once again—is to create your own work and act! You are more attractive as a possible client when you are acting in something that an agent or casting director can see you in. Another concern is that when you finally do meet with an agent, she will ask you if you have a five-minute demo reel that showcases your talent. If you don't have any, what can you do? Film has changed dramatically with the advent of the digital movie camera. For only a few hundred dollars and with an editing program on your computer, you can make your own short movie. By investing in yourself, writing a scene that highlights your talent, and creating your own work, you have the ability to produce your own reel. You can always tell the prospective agent that this work is a low-budget independent movie currently in production, which is absolutely true! By using your creativity and remaining proactive, you build for yourself a broader avenue through which to be discovered. Another way to find film work is to frequent the casting bulletin boards at film schools. There are numerous bright and creative young filmmakers looking for actors to collaborate with. The more experience you have acting on film, the better prepared you will be when a paying professional job comes along.

Another part of the process of getting started as an actor is to go and watch other actors work. If the work is interesting and exciting, you'll learn by example. You'll notice how they solve a moment by making a creative choice that you hadn't thought of. Watching a friend have a breakthrough in her work can inspire you to keep at it yourself. You may discover a writer whose prose excites your imagination as if he were speaking directly to you. Even when the work is uninteresting, there is value in asking yourself what the actors could do differently to improve their performance. Always go and support your friends when they are acting. Surround yourself with a handful of individuals whom you can rely on to tell you the truth about your work. (When I was a young actor, we would all go out after a show to a neighborhood bar and endlessly discuss the work.) Learn how to talk about your craft in a positive way. It was my ability to help my friends with constructive suggestions in a nurturing manner that led me to become an acting teacher as well as a director. It was something I had never thought of, but through the encouragement of others, a door opened for me.

Remember, getting started means just that—a place to begin. It might take you years before you actually start getting paid to act. As long as you find meaning in this adventure, keep at it with your heart and soul. Check in periodically to make sure you remain active in your pursuit. Look to act whenever the opportunity presents itself, and dare I say yet again, create your own opportunities!

Steve Vinovich: We all get in it for the art, for the fun, for the play. They don't teach you in school what to do in the real world. They teach you how to speak and how to do period dance in Juilliard. Then they throw you out there. You kind of land and look around, what do I do? Then you find out there's *Backstage*, a newspaper that has all the auditions that week and you can go and audition for them. Then you find out sort of through other people how to get to agents and send them your picture and résumé—all of that to get an agent. I've been pretty lucky. I kind of fell into it right away in New York. Though I did go out for many things through *Backstage*. Today you look at *Breakdowns* and try to find out how to get work. They taught you a lot about the craft of theater but not about the business. I think they are doing more of that these days than they used to because people our age now have come in and say, "Why aren't they teaching that?" You know a lot of them do bring in professionals. I student teach sometimes, I guest artist six, seven times. I bring in what a résumé looks like. I bring in my reel, this is what a reel is. I tell them, you need commercial agents, you need regular agents. What you want to do with a manager. What that costs you, or can. You have to get pictures, you have to get different pictures. You might want a straight picture and you want a commercial picture. This is just sort of the basics, but you're never taught the basics in school.

Gregory Itzin: It didn't happen right away by any means. I kind of thought it would. The first agent I had took me because I was from ACT [American Conservatory Theater] and sort of expected me to use that cachet myself. Let me preface all this by saying, I'm not as an individual tremendously ambitious. By that I mean, the trappings of ambition. I am ambitious in the work that I do. I remember when I first started out I was so naïve. I remember the first pilot I did. They asked me in the interview what I wanted to be. I said I wanted to be a star, of course. I was twenty-something, I was young. I think now I know better. I don't want to be a star. I want to be a recognized working actor. I guess I sort of am that. You always end up wanting something more. Even the people who have the most want more, I suppose. It took a long time. First I started doing costars. One-day jobs. One-day jobs with billing way down the line. Costar, whatever that is. You start small. Usually for most people, unless there is something about you, you're blessed with that quirk, then you'll be typed as that thing. But if you're just a good, competent actor, most of the things that I ended up with at first were information characters. Doctors that told you that your son was this or the cop at the desk who says, "Right that way, ma'am," where you start small. The first time you get a part you can sink your teeth in, you get a little bigger. For me I had to imagine the next step. And that was by dint of going out and doing it, going out and doing it. Getting the job, OK, I know I can do that. Then I had to get it a couple of times, to really know that I was capable of being the guest star. For me that was a slow process. Some people I think . . . eat it up right away. Some people are eaten up right away. I think women have a much harder time than men. It took—what am I, fifty-something now, and I've been here since I was thirty. That's twenty-some years. It's taken, I would say, the first five or six years to get rolling.

Lupe Ontiveros: I worked as an extra a couple of times. I was an extra in *The World's Greatest Lover*. The extras I played were little hookers. I did *The Border* with [Jack] Nicholson, countless numbers of extra roles. Then I got my feet wet. I had to bamboozle my way into the Screen Actors Guild. I actually started with AFTRA [American Federation of Television and Radio Artists]. But I started doing plays, Latino plays. I found a guy who was producing a show in Spanish and I said, "I'm a beginning actress and I got to get into the union." But we know it's a Catch-22. It never makes any sense to me. You can't get a job because you're not a union member, and you can't get into the union because you don't have a job. I was between those professions [social worker and actor] and trying to make a decision as to what my life was going to be about. Shortly after that I started going out for roles.

Shannon Kenny: I saved up all my money and I wanted to go to theater school. I auditioned for theater school in Australia [her home]. There is only one theater school, National Theater School of Dramatic Arts, and I didn't get in. A year later I went back thinking I was going to get in because I got really close that time out of high school. A year later I was less close getting in, so I decided to go to England or America. I ended [up] coming to the States. I was late for auditioning and the only school I got to audition for was Cal Arts [California Institute for the Arts], and I got in. In the interim I actually auditioned for Juilliard too and got in as well. I had to decide between the two. I stuck with Cal Arts and that is where I ended up going.

Mary Pat Gleason: I walked dogs and cleaned houses for years. [*laughs*] I got involved in Off-Off-Broadway theater. Then I got a break. A dear friend of mine whose house I cleaned—two friends I cleaned their houses—were writers. They wrote soap operas. I was cleaning their house one day and they said, "Mary Pat, what are you doing here?" I said, "What am I doing here? I'm cleaning your house." They said, "You should be doing film and television." I said, "That's why I'm actually here. But I haven't been able to crack that." They said, "You should be doing it and we are going to see that you do." A year later I was working a regional theater and I got a phone call and these guys had written a part for me on *Texas* [a soap opera]. I came in and auditioned for a hooker; that's what I was playing. They then just kept writing me. They covered themselves in a future episode, saying I was an undercover cop when I was a hooker. Then I became an undercover cop; then I became the cleaning lady in the house the marshal ran. [*laughs*]

Randle Mell: I was very fearful. I did a lot of plays in high school, but when I graduated from high school I became very insecure and fearful. I remember my father telling me that this new program opened up at the Juilliard School. I was living in New Jersey at the time. It was a brand-new program, a serious acting program at the Juilliard School. And I remember my father bringing me this article about it. I remember wanting it but being just too damned frightened to move to New York City and commit. So I basically spent about five years, six years, bumming around, going to college, quitting college. Working at the Bucks County Playhouse as an apprentice for a year. Traveling across country, ending up in Santa Barbara and going to school. Eventually when I graduated from UC–Santa Barbara, I said, "All right, it's do or die." I auditioned for the Juilliard School and got in. Then my path was set. I completed the program and just started working from there.

Michael Paul Chan: A lot [of] false starts and stops. I took a theater class in state college, which was very foreign and turned me off. I then tried community theater because it was familiar to me. I became a founding member of an Asian American theater company in San Francisco. I started thinking if I was going to do this seriously, I better get some serious training. I went to ACT and got a partial scholarship. After two years I felt I was in way over my head. I was up against kids who were MFAs in theater. A lot of the instructors there [at ACT] thought there wasn't a place for you in the American theater. By that time I was married and we decided to move to L.A. and then I got involved with the East West Players.

April Grace: We were living in Louisiana—my father was in the air force—we were on our way to Saudi Arabia. It turned out I got to choose any high school I wanted to go to in Europe. I started thinking about acting; I decided to go to London. I thought, if I do the acting thing, London would be a good place to be. I went to London, Central High School, but in the back of my mind [I was] thinking, I should not be an actor because I need to pay for things. I need to make a living and that was going to be very difficult—so maybe I'll do the right thing and become a lawyer. I was doing all the theater programs in high school and then divine intervention stepped in. I was being courted by a lot of universities and one of the letters I got in the mail said, "Dear Negro student," on it. When that letter came to me, I said to myself, "I'm going to last five minutes in this kind of environment with these kinds of people." I remember running back to the dorm to call my parents. "Mom, I just got this letter in the mail that said, 'Dear Negro student' on it, what is going on? I can't do it!" That was when the decision was flushed in my head. A couple of weeks after that, I saw Terrance Stamp in *Dracula* and it blew my mind. That nailed it down for me.

Andrew Prine: I left my picture in an agent's office. On my way out—uninvited, of course—I stumbled over a chair by the secretary's desk. Literally fell on my face as the agent was walking through to her office. I left in embarrassment. Four days later she called me—I didn't have an agent—and they had a role for me in an army Signal Corps film in Queens, Long Island, about a young clumsy boy in the army. [*laughs*] They gave it to me, they just gave it to me. I made a hundred and fifty dollars and it cost two hundred dollars to get into the Screen Actors Guild.

Robert Picardo: We did a production of the [Leonard] Bernstein *Mass* at Yale with people from the Yale community and students. All of a sudden I was working with young amateur actors who were my peers or perhaps in my class. But also older people from the community, because that piece required people of different ages. Leonard Bernstein came to see it. It was a big success within the university. He said, "I want this production to represent my piece in Europe." So we got to take this to Vienna and perform this. I had a featured role in it. Mr. Bernstein was very kind to me. He paid me a compliment: "You have genuine energy on stage, not phony Broadway energy. What are your ambitions? What do you want to do with your life?" I said, "I plan to go to medical school." He said, "You should think about doing this. You have real energy—that's real stage energy." That's what I remember him saying. I looked him in the eye and I said, "Tell my mother." [*laughs*] When my mother came up to the opening I brought her over to Leonard Bernstein and he basically said, "I think your son is talented; he should think of becoming a performer." I knew that was one of the only ways I was going to get myself off of that premed track. To have someone that important and that validated say, "I think your son should consider this possible career choice," was a very important step in my taking it seriously.

Emily Kuroda: When I was in grammar school I was known as the child who didn't talk. In high school I started doing humorous and dramatic interpretation and I started directing. In college I was a drama major—my academic adviser told me I had to go into education because I was Asian American. I guess they thought being an actor was absurd.

I got my master's in theater and education and did my student teaching and I hated it. Then East West Players [Asian American Theater Company] came to Cal State–Fresno, where I was going. I saw people who were actually actors and were Asian American. I came down to Los Angeles just to take classes for the summer and I have stayed ever since.

Julio Oscar Mechoso: Andy [Garcia] is a real buddy of mine, came to get me at the airport [in Los Angeles]. He helped me find a place—introduced me to a lot of casting directors—whenever he could he'd get me an audition. Plus his advice helped me work on my first reel. Andy got me an audition for *Internal Affairs.* Andy has got a lot of friends, he got all his friends auditions. Andy is good to all his friends. But I was so ready, so inspired. Andy arranged for the director [Mike Figgis] to meet all of us directly at this meeting—for the director to make the decisions. Andy said, "Go in there and do your best in that role. He is already in love with a character actor who has done a lot of stuff." I said, "OK." Andy said, "I'll get you a role where you say one line, I'll get you something." I got ready for that shit, brother. [*laughs*] I walked into the audition room and before we start, I tell the director, "Let me tell you something. I don't give a fuck who you give this role to, but nobody in this cast loves Andy Garcia more than I do." I just went at it, tears were coming down. I did the scene. I walked out of that room, I saw all of Andy's friends, and I said to myself, "You guys are fucked. You ain't going to do what I did there." Less than twenty-four hours [later], Andy calls, "What the fuck did you do in that audition? The director is dropping so and so and they are going with you." I walked in and told the truth.

Marcella Lowery: It wasn't until I moved to New York that I saw all the theater that I could. I read all the plays I could. It was like I was starved out there. I never had it. Every play I got my hands on, I read. Since black theater was a little bit more alive and happening then—New Dramatists, Ellen Stewart—there were tons of plays to see. I met Hattie Winston, who was involved in the Negro Ensemble Company—she first invited me to a Robert Hooks [an actor] workshop—she invited the actors in that group to join the Negro Ensemble Company. I saw plays in [Central] Park. Everything I could see, everything I could read, that's what I did. For each play I saw that I liked, it gave me more energy and more courage to carry on. Remember we were in the civil rights movement, so

I had something to prove. You got your shot, then you were reminded this isn't all about you. You're standing on some shoulders here, don't go out there and be a fool. You weren't allowed to fail. You were representing everyone who had worked hard so you would have that opportunity. It wasn't about messing up, you had obligations. I hate to use it—to be a credit to your race—may sound really dated now—but basically that is what you had to do. It was the civil rights movement and everybody had to carry their own load and do their own share. If you fell down you got up again and kept going. No excuses, no complaints, you just kept going. That was it. You did it with pride and integrity because you had something to prove.

John Rothman: I wanted to take on New York. It was very daunting. One thing that I did find was taking [acting] class was very useful. Not only in Michael [Howard] did you have a great teacher, you were surrounded by other actors trying to figure it out. You began to have a sense of community. I studied with Austin [Pendelton] at HB [Studio] for a time. I took singing lessons in New York. I took Rosemary Tichler's audition class because I had very little experience in auditioning. All this made you feel like you were part of a community. Plus you do a piece of work in class and it works and it's good—you get positive reinforcement—that makes you feel stronger to go out. I also realized I would have to have an agent. That was a priority. Coming out of Yale was a big advantage. I got an agent very quickly from auditioning in an agent's office. Jeff Hunter [an agent] would send me out for a lot [of] things I didn't get. I thought, "How long was this going to last? How long is this guy going to send me out when I don't get a job?" There was a lot of learning from making mistakes.

Roxanne Hart: I really think that phrase, "Fools walk in where wise men fear to tread," really applied to me. I was very fearless. Maybe it had something to do with having nothing to lose. Everybody told me the way to get an agent was to do commercials. So I got this book, agents by building [that contains addresses of all the New York agents by building], you have your little 8 by 10 [headshot] and you go around. You go into these buildings, these different agencies, and you go with your picture. You go up on the elevator. They would have this sign, "Leave your picture in the box." I would pick up all the pictures and I would go in. I would just start engaging someone in conversation. I would force my way in. I did that at the Public Theater [New York Shakespeare Festival]. I waited around for hours. I would sit outside [casting director] Rosemary Tichler's office and ask her if she wanted coffee, that I was going across the street. It just sort of amazes me [that I did that]; I didn't have anything to lose.

Nestor Carbonell: I knew as soon as I got out here [Los Angeles] what was really important was having tape [a demo reel]. I didn't have much. Generally people don't want to read you and they don't want to make the effort to go see a play all the time. You get [the] odd exceptional agent that does. Business works much faster. Nowadays because we have enough technology with digital cameras—you can get a high-definition camera that's really small—you can shoot a scene or a whole movie for next to nothing. You can be part of a production that doesn't need a huge name because the cost of shooting a film can be so cheap. There are fewer and fewer excuses for [not] getting tape nowadays. That is something actors should really take advantage of as early as they can. Do as many movies as they can on digital.

Rif Hutton: There was an actor by the name of Dolph Sweet—I worked with him in San Francisco at the Cannery doing *Streamers*—he had a TV series in L.A. I wound up doing an under-five [a role with five lines or less] and I said, "Dolph, L.A. is kicking my ass." He said, "Are you doing the theater?" I said, "Yeah I'm out there cranking." He said, "Are you sending out postcards?" "Yeah." "How about pictures and résumés, cover letters?" I said, "Yeah but I'm not getting any response." He said, "Send them certified—make them sign for them." I said, "That's going to piss them off." He said, "Be polite but be insistent." He gave me a whole talk and the central message of it was if you truly believe you are the best product available, then you have to be willing to go the extra mile to push that product out there so people find out about your product. You can't say, they are going to come and find me, you have to shove yourself in front of their face. Not to do it in a rude way, [just] make sure you get out there in front of them.

Lee Garlington: I knew if I didn't give this thing a shot I would always regret it. I gave myself ten years. I came out here [Los Angeles] and I said if when I'm thirty-five I'm not able to make a living, that's still young enough to go to college, get a degree, and have a whole other career. When I did my first play [at Equity Theater in L.A.] that ran for five months, Jackie Birch [a casting director] waited afterwards—in some little rinky-dink, fucking-hole-in-the wall place. She comes up to me and says, "I really liked what you did. Who's your agent?" I said, "I don't have one." She brought me in for an audition on a movie called *Psycho II*, which I got. She negotiated my contract for me. She sent me up with five agents. She made the calls for me. If you can get somebody in the business to champion you, a director, a casting director, somebody who can make those calls to an agent's office, there is no better way to get started. I got my first agent through her, which I was with for five minutes. Then I went with another agent that I have been with my entire career.

Ashley Gardner: I went to New York with everybody else and we had the League [of Professional Schools] auditions at the end of our graduating year. All the producers, directors, agents would come to see each class do scenes. Fortunately I got an agent out of that right after school. I know a lot of people in my class never got an agent and never got going because there were no opportunities for them. I kind of had a year where I floundered. Stayed up late, drinking coffee, watching *Mary Tyler Moore* reruns, feeling kind of depressed. Absolutely not knowing what to do when I got there. Then I got a job. I remember thinking that unless I do something about this, I am just going to end [up] like a lot of people who go to New York, get discouraged, and then go home. After the first three months when I didn't become the big star they [first agent] thought I was going to become, they stopped sending me out. It took me nine months to figure out somebody had to work for me. It couldn't be me going to cattle calls. So I fired them. I ended up calling the other agents that were interested in me. A year later it was "no, no." One guy, Kenny Kaplan, said, "I remember you, come on in."

Clyde Kusatsu: I wound up hooking up with the East West Players, the nation's first Asian American theater company. I found a niche there for about nine years. I didn't care, because I was a working actor. By being a working actor, that means I get paid $17.50 per performance for a children's show. So I'm considered a working actor. At one time I lived in the back of the theater. I was the janitor. The title was the BME—the building maintenance engineer. Whenever I would get a gig, say a guest star, I'd come back and mop the floor, clean the toilets, get ready for the night's performance. Theater parties would have catered food; I'd save some and be in the kitchen. As long as I had some food and enough for beer, I was happy. I was studying becoming a dedicated actor.

Ethan Phillips: I was so driven, so determined. I was not going to fail at this. I had blinders on and I lived and I slept, ate, and I breathed acting since I decided to do this. I never really worried about the business. Everybody in New York was worried about 8 by 10s and résumés—can I get this agent, what about this casting director? I would pick up *Show Business* [a trade paper] and find a play. I'd go and audition and get a role in some stupid little Off-Off-Broadway theater. I always maintained that if you did good work, you would create fire. That fire would blossom into smoke and people would see that smoke and they would come and find you. I did six, seven, eight, nine shows, the accumulation of which made me better as an actor. I also sowed seeds with people who would hire me in the future and I got an agent out of that.

CHAPTER THREE

Passion, Process, and Perseverance

An actor with *passion* has one of the three necessary elements that form the groundwork for sustaining your life's chosen work. The other two building blocks are *process* and *perseverance*. When you combine your passion for acting with a reliable way of working and an absolute determination to stick it out, you have established a foundation that will support you throughout your professional life. When actors develop a proven technique that gives them access to their instrument, they make themselves more likely to find work. If your work is hit-or-miss, or you try to get by solely on your intuition (which can take you only so far), then you rob yourself of the gift of craft as well as a dependable way to solve the challenges in a play or script. An actor with a proven process and a firm grasp of her craft will be able to keep going and growing in this profession. Now add to this winning combination a strength of will. When you add that part of yourself that supplies you with the necessary courage to remain faithful in your pursuit, you have the makings of an actor with *passion, process,* and *perseverance.*

An actor must continue his studies with an experienced acting teacher if he is to grow as an actor and maximize working potential. The questions actors then need to ask of themselves are: "What am I trying to accomplish by going to acting class?" and "What commitment am I willing to make to achieve that goal?" With a wide range of respected acting teachers to choose from, what criteria should you use when deciding whom to study with? When I have an initial meeting with a prospective student, I occasionally use the following analogy to describe the importance of process. A violin is a beautiful four-stringed musical instrument that takes years of practice to fully express its lyrical possibilities. A musician would not be able to call herself a true violinist unless she knew how to play all the strings. An actor is her own instrument, her own unique Stradivarius violin. If you are to be as good an actor as you possibly can, it would be foolish and counterproductive not to learn how to pluck all of your strings and use them in your work. That will mean that at times you will have to go to places inside of yourself that may feel uncomfortable or dangerous because they are challenging to your sense of self. Many actors, when forced to confront this part of themselves, flee out of fear. They try to rationalize away the true importance of going beneath the surface. Those who are brave enough to meet this challenge open themselves up to infinitely more artistic possibilities. This makes you a more interesting actor, one who exhibits a deeper commitment to seeking the truth in your work. That is the type of actor that colleagues respect and audiences want to pay good money to see.

The most important element in choosing an acting teacher is to find someone whom you can trust. First and foremost, this individual must be able to communicate with you in a manner that is both nurturing and challenging, and this must take place in a safe environment. An open and available actor sitting down in a chair in front of his peers after acting in a scene, monologue, or acting exercise is in a vulnerable position. A good acting coach must understand who you are and know which buttons to push (and which not to) to help you make the necessary personal discoveries. A wise acting coach becomes an inspirational mentor who opens you up to your own creativity. As an actor you want to know it is safe for you to fail in a class without the pressures of having to perform. You want to be sure that your individual needs as an artist will be met. If it's possible for you to audit a class before signing up, observe how the coach relates to the actors and how the actors talk to one another. Don't let "celebrity" students, past or present, sway your thinking. A teacher who may or may not be deservedly in vogue may not be the right person for you. Acting class should be a private matter for all those involved. It is not a place for agents, managers, or industry folk to be observers. Trust your intuition. Some questions to ask yourself:

- Do I respect the actors who are working in this class?
- Does the acting coach share insight into the actors' work, or does he spend too much time talking about himself?
- Do I believe there is integrity in the room and actors' work to admire?
- Is there a sense of comradeship among the actors? Are they willing to network and be mutually supportive of one another?

- Will the acting coach come and see my work? Does she make herself easily accessible to speak with?

I firmly believe that when an actor has chosen a class, she has to be willing to make a long-term commitment to that teacher and class in order to get any value out of it. If there are struggles—and there will be—you must work them out in class. There are no six-week how-to classes to acting success. When you develop a reliable technique, you can adapt it to whatever material or situation you will be performing in. A well-trained actor with a solid grasp of his craft knows how to audition and how to act in commercials, on stage, in motion pictures, and in episodic television. The responsibility lies with you to be working in class. Bring in scenes, monologues, and acting exercises that stimulate your imagination. Look for challenging roles and authors that stretch you as an artist, roles you might not ever actually be cast in. Acting class is your chance to express your inner life as you continue to unfold as a human being, to explore roles and writers you might not otherwise have the chance to.

Unless you are extremely lucky—and I wouldn't try to build a career on luck alone—you will have to persevere. Perseverance cannot be taught and you will have to experience for yourself how ambitious you are if you will have any chance of success. The foundation of passion and process is nothing without the personal determination of the individual. There are too many other actors willing to do whatever it takes to succeed. No matter how many times the door is slammed in their faces, they go back at it again and again and again. Those who don't develop a tough skin, who can't handle the rejection, missed opportunities, and long periods of unemployment, are not cut out for the professional acting world. That is the cold, hard truth. So, then, how does this foundation stay strong? How do you not lose hope when having to confront so large an obstacle? Passion, process, and perseverance have to play off one another to be constantly mutually supportive. When your desire for all three is great enough, it remains the foundation and reason to continue. Every cliché you can think of holds true. If at first you don't succeed, try, try again. What doesn't break you only makes you stronger. Or in the words of Winston Churchill, "Never give up. Never. Never. Never." There will be times for you as an actor when the struggle seems insurmountable. That will be a good time for you to go back to your foundation and search within, to see if you still have the resolve to continue. You'll need a network of family and friends to encourage you to keep trying. You must believe that in spite of the difficulty at hand, there is a place for you if you remain steadfast.

From my own experience I have discovered that perseverance is a spiritual journey. How much you can endure becomes a personal matter. The journey of the working actor is about this discovery. The preeminent scholar Joseph Campbell writes in his book *The Power of Myth* (1988) of the heroic journey we take in life if we so choose, asserting that in our quest for knowledge, we are tested by inner and outward forces. As actors we are challenged as the hero in our own journey to constantly find ways to battle these obstacles and to find significance for ourselves. By searching for meaning and discovering the courage to remain resolute, we become our own mythic hero in the journey of the working actor. Clearly some will decide to move on to some other profession, as they should, while others will struggle endlessly for an elusive goal. But those with talent, who remain honest with themselves, and view the obstacles as opportunities, will be the ones with passion, process, and perseverance and will use this as a spiritual journey of personal and artistic discoveries.

John P. Connolly: Here's my early training: none! I had no early training. None whatsoever. Consciously rejected it. Refused to take an acting class, a voice class, a singing class, a dance class, a movement class. Any kind of class. Absolutely and utterly rejected it! Pride goeth before a fall. Because it struck me that the strength I had as a performer was a gift from God. That I was able to live my life extempore from my mother wit. And that included my work on stage. And it was all about the kind of energy, immediacy, improvisatory ability, and brains that I could bring to bear on [the] work. And it had nothing to do with any kind of formal training, which I was absolutely and utterly convinced, being twenty years old, would do nothing but inhibit my ability to act. Until the first six times I completely lost my voice in the middle of a run, I thought I was right. [*laughs*] So, I absolutely would take no training at all. It wasn't until I bashed up against the wall—the brick wall of the limits of impulse and ingenuity—that I had to really face the fact that there was something systematic. A formal approach to the work that I better explore if this was going to be my life's work.

Lisa Blake Richards: First I worked with Stella Adler and then I worked with someone who taught the Method. Then I worked at the Actors Studio from about 1968 on. I really felt that the training I got— honest, honest, honest!—I feel it works for everything. People don't tend to not use it. For me when I get a part, I love it whether it's on television or on the stage or anywhere. I feel that I use the same technique really. There are people who take these classes for television class or take a class in how to do a commercial or how to do a sitcom [situation comedy]. I feel it's all bullshit really. Because if you act, you act! [Lee] Strassberg once told me, "Lisa, you cannot work the way the English work. You cannot work outward, in. It does not work for you. Just forget it." I always find I have to do a lot more preparation than anyone I know. To learn my lines, to deal with my character, to relax. Otherwise I'm nervous and miserable. But if I do all the work, the sensory work, the background, what I would wear on a certain day, if I do all of that work and create that world, then I feel good.

Andrew Prine: For two years I was on Broadway doing *Look Homeward, Angel* in the leading role. I learned how to act during that time. I had no discipline. George Roy Hill [the director] almost beat me to death in the rehearsals because he could not get the same performance out of me twice as we rehearsed. I had no real knowledge of that kind of thing. I had never run more than a week in a summer stock play. [*laughs*] I had no discipline and I was arrogant. I had the arrogance of youth and ignorance. No one could tell me anything. I am embarrassed to say how ignorant I was. He had to keep on me very hard. For two years almost every night the stage manager who had instructions came back with notes—to keep me on track, so I knew where the beats were, I knew where the laughs were, which were terribly important in this tragic, emotional show—we needed the few laughs that we had. I would start improving it after four performances and he'd come and take out the improvements. I literally learned how to really act in that show. I was only going on my talent, and that's not enough. It was an undisciplined, rebellious talent.

James Rebhorn: I came to Columbia University and got my MFA. It was there that my understanding of acting took on a whole new meaning. Up until that time I wasn't really aware that there was actually a craft or a system behind acting. I thought you sort of just read the script and just did it. You kind of let your imagination feed you, which is still very important. You pursue an action, you pursue an objective, you break down a scene. There's actually some craft involved in it. I sort of fell in love with the craft aspect of it. I can break it down, break down a script. That I can make choices. I can come into a room and ask, "Why is this night different from all other nights? What's the urgency?" All the stuff kind of excited me. I remember the first time getting to do a scene—and it was just not me, this was his [acting teacher Ted Kasanoff] response to everybody. You would open your mouth and start speaking and he would say, "What are you doing?" [*laughs*] "I'm doing this." He'd say, "No, no, no, what are you doing?" I said, "I'm doing this scene." He said, "No, *what are you doing?*" My love of the craft came from that.

Hal Landon: I did pretty much act by instinct for a long time. When we moved to this larger theater and these other actors started to come in, I started to play smaller parts. I got pushed into pushing [forcing the acting work for a result], literally playing for effects, indicating, whatever you want to call it. It shames me to say it now, but that was what I was doing. To try and match this higher level. I was playing Teach in *American Buffalo*, great part and I wasn't making it. So I thought, what was I going to do here? It was quit or get better. I decided to study a technique. I was always attracted to Michael Chekhov's book *To the Actor*. I found there was a guy up in L.A., George Shdanoff, who the book is actually dedicated to, and he was teaching classes. I studied with him pretty intensively for four years. I found a technique and a way of working transformed me. I got a whole different perspective of my sense of truth.

Lauren Tom: I really studied—I poured all of that energy and angst into going to class. I was going to dancing, singing, and acting classes. I was nineteen years old and I was kind of able to deal with living in New York City with not a lot of money. I think the only way to do it is if you are young. If you have such a passion and a love for it and you've got some youth on your side, I think the chances of you making it are going to be really high. You have to be the best possible artist that you can be and do as many things as possible. That's why I was training in those three areas. If it was slow in the acting, I could do a dance, industrial-dance in a little show with Gregory Hines and sell dance wear. That's what enabled me to keep working all the time. Being Asian, being ethnic, being five feet tall, I wasn't going to be getting a lot of jobs in the chorus line of other shows. I knew I was going to have to find something that was special about myself and get behind that and push.

Gregory Itzin: ACT is a school that teaches—I am pretty sure it still does—[a] classical acting program. It was like turning loose a kid in a candy store, for me, 'cause I had done all sorts of stuff. I never had any formal training at the University of Wisconsin. I never really remember being taught a method or anything else. When I got to San Francisco, when I got to ACT, it was like a kid in a candy store. I got taught Stanislavski method, Uta Hagen's method. I got taught mime, ballet, and modern dance and fencing. How to create a character from the inside out, how to create a character from the outside in. Different classes taught different things. Dialects, we got Shakespeare, specifically Shakespeare classes. Text work. It was a golden opportunity and I just swam in it. I just loved it. I had a great time.

Emily Kuroda: I had a very supportive teacher in college, Dr. Loring, and she said that she thought she saw something in me. That gave me the courage to pursue it. I had this really small part in *Two Gentlemen of Verona* and during theater history class, she said, "I can't take my eyes off Emily Kuroda." No one had ever said that to me before. That still stays with me because that was the moment that gave me the courage to defy all the other professors in college. Mako [an acting teacher with East West Players] taught me to really listen to the other person. Listening to the other person, the give-and-take, the trusting in yourself and of the other person. You do all this homework and right before you go on, you wipe the slate clean—it's like skydiving, you don't know where you are going to go. Every time it's different. Your homework will come out in different ways. It's scary and it's a thrill; it could fail miserably, but that's what I got out of my years with him.

Kevin Bourland: I found the best training I got, that I still use now—that I rely on, it helps me whether it's drama or comedy—is my improvisational background at the Groundlings. That was the best training any actor can get. The audition process is different than the acting-class process. It is almost like a one eighty. You prepare for it, but once you are there, on the dime something else is expected of you. Quick adjustments; listening is key to the casting director, the director. When you shoot it is the same kind of situation. There is no time. Improvisation helped me to think on my feet, respond quicker, listen sharply, invent. When the wheels fall off you have to figure how to drive the car with no wheels. I found it a much more exciting way to act. To discover.

Lucinda Jenney: What acting class was able to do for me was to confirm me to myself. I wasn't sure. I thought I was doing it right, I had a lot of belief in myself based on instinct, love, and he [acting teacher Michael Howard] reflected that back to me. Yes, I was on the right track. Yes, I could do this. Then he gave me insight through exercises, relaxation to figure out how to use my strengths. Discover my weaknesses, strengthen my weaknesses, and move on.

Lupe Ontiveros: I think every actor should take a class of psychology. We are psychologists to a large degree. We take a character and we analyze that character. The more you understand about life, the better an actor you can be in the profoundness of what needs to be there. That's where you get all that texture. It's just the getting it out that's the difficult part. My background and my eighteen years in social work gave me all that insight that I now share with my roles.

Mary Pat Gleason: That would be New York, oh my God! I was cleaning houses, walking dogs, waiting tables. A couple of the waiters that I was waiting tables with were really dynamic personalities and fun. We would have a fabulous time together. One of them, Michael Patrick King, who is the producer-director—Emmy Award–winning director, I might add—of *Sex and the City*. We started an improv group. We really sustained ourselves on nothing. We had so little money. I remember the nights that we would just, we'd all pool coins that we had, five bucks among us. We would walk from Seventy-Second Street all the way down to Little Italy. We'd have dinner at Chinatown because we [could] afford a couple of dishes. We'd have dessert and coffee in Little Italy and walk all the way home. That was our Saturday night. And they were fabulous. None of us even thought for a second that we were in a difficult situation.

We moaned. We moaned about someday people we were cleaning for were going to have to pay seventy-five dollars to come to see us on stage. So we did that, because we had so much support. I can't stress that more for young people. To find people that you care about and care about them through thick and thin. Because they are going to be your friends for life. And those friendships will sustain you when your heart fails you. Or when you've been rejected many times and then you've got that one friend who keeps reminding you that you have a spark. That you have a gift. That's what we are here for. To really buoy one another up when those times happen. And they happen. There's no way around them.

Erick Avari: It took me three years to get my Equity card. I think that was my biggest slog in my early years. Going from one dreadful show-case after the next. Praying that it would somehow move Off Broadway and I'd get my card. That was the next hurdle and I figured once I get there, it's going to be smooth sailing. But of course it never is. You do tackle one obstacle at a time. Those were the most effort in terms of perseverance because there was no paycheck at the end of the day and it looked so bleak. That's when you start to look around and see the number of actors just falling by the wayside and then the reality starts to sink in. I could perhaps very easily be one of those guys. I figured I had come all this way and I wasn't going to let go. [*laughs*] I just loved it so much. I was able to do a lot of other jobs, survival jobs—and the only thing that got me through it was knowing that I had a rehearsal after or a performance; then I could endure whatever they wanted me to do during the day. As long as I got my fix of the theater, I felt that was enough for me. If I let that go I was going to let go of a huge part of my life.

Juanita Jennings: I think that's where faith comes in. For me I have a very strong belief in the Lord. So I don't worry about a lot of things. Don't do this if you want to be a star. You do it because you love it. It's what makes you sing. I have a family. I love my family first and foremost. It's like a painter—a painter has to paint, a sculptor has to sculpt, a pianist has to play. I do that because I love to play. There are all kinds of ways to keep yourself going. I keep coming back to that theater thing. Getting together with people who are writing scripts. Reading for them.

It's like religion in a sense. You do it, you go to service, because that's what you believe, or that's what makes you feel. I'm not giving up. This is what I do.

Marcella Lowery: A lot of people are going to tell you no, but there will be somebody who'll say, "Let's give her a shot." Because you keep doing it. I think people give up too easily, especially the younger generation. They want it quick and fast and now. There is no working up towards it, they just want it. We're going to be rappers, [we're] going to get a hit record, it's just going to happen. There is something that has happened out here where you want it quick. People don't think you have to pay dues anymore. I think you appreciate it more when you pay dues. It's not so fleeting because you earned it, you worked for it. That's a good feeling, that's the durable part of it.

Debra Monk: I was working as a waitress [on and off for four years] and I met some other friends who were out of work as well. We started thinking of writing something. I had never written anything. This girlfriend of mine and I got together—I've been working as a waitress—I find them fascinating—I'd like to write about those women. So we started writing about waitresses. She was a great singer, my background was acting, so we thought we could do some songs—she could help me with the singing and I could help her with the acting. We wrote this piece that had songs in it. Her husband was also working on a piece about gas station attendants. What happened was we merged together and became *Pump Boys and Dinettes*. At the time none of us could afford our rent—I remember I was paying off my college, which was very expensive, and I had to not work as much in order to write this piece. I remember I called my brother and asked if he could help me out with the rent and my payment that month. I said, I promise I'll pay you back, and I did. I could have dropped out of the group, saying, I can't do this, I have to work. But I didn't.

Rif Hutton: I got out to Oakland and very quickly went through the little bit of money that I had. I was homeless. At that time I was living in Berkley, California. All of my worldly possessions were in this barrel that I left in storage at the airport because I didn't have a real home address. I burned through my cash [paying for a hotel near People's Park] and there was the Rialto Movie Theater right next door to that hotel. Before they kicked me out of that hotel, I looked out the window and saw the rooftop. I said, "That's shelter." I got a cardboard box and climbed up the back wall and that was my home for a while. I would get my meals at the Berkley Free Clinic—if you helped serve each meal, you got twenty-five cents, which gave me bus fare to go out to auditions. Every seven days I would give blood at the blood clinic and that would give me some money. That's how I kept rolling. Fortunately in Berkley there was such a community of people in similar circumstances as me I never felt that I was in terrible shape or that this is the end of me, the end of my life. It was just part of the adventure. I felt 100 percent confident that once I auditioned for OAT [Oakland Actors Theater] that I was going to get in the company and move on from there.

Sheila Kelley: I started acting in New York because I was a dancer. I had gone to NYU to be a dance major but I had an injury and I had to quit, so I became an acting major. I hated acting at that point. I just didn't like all the rules, all the crap. I left the acting program and found Michael Howard [acting teacher]. I was very, very young and he said, "We don't take people as young as you." I was very persistent and I said, "OK, I'll study with Peter Thompson," who was next door in the same studio. So I studied with Peter and every time I saw Michael, I'd say, "Hi, Michael. How are you? I'm only nineteen but I really want to study with you." So within six months he invited me into his class. I started with Michael at the age of nineteen. Michael was such a liberating experience because there is such a freedom in that particular technique. You can bring everything to the table—there aren't all these rules that I had found—so it really freed my instrument up.

Shannon Kenny: What kept me going was all that fierce ambition. That thing that started me when I was nine, that wanting to be famous. That single-minded kind of drive above [all] else. You can't leave your country [Australia] and do this without that. Ultimately that ambition, it's so funny, has faded. That was what kept me going through those miserable depressing times. I learned it a little later that I should have had a life outside of that [showbiz]. Though that drive is what keeps you going. It's a really weird balance you have to strive for.

Julio Oscar Mechoso: I was a private investigator, car repossessor for a long time [in Miami]. I was always doing theater at nights and always auditioning. I'd like to have jobs that gave me room to move. As a private investigator and a car repossessor, I set up my own time. If I was doing a play or a little gig somewhere I'd say, I'm not available. When I came over [to L.A.], I was a substitute teacher for a long time. Subbing, you can call in and say you are unavailable. Any job I took anybody knew that once they called me for an audition, I was gone. In the back of my head I always had this thing: I can make it. I know I can do it. So I never put myself in the position that I was totally out of the running.

Ethan Phillips: This really illustrates how important it is just to show up. The Actors Fest was basically seventeen nights in a row, ten actors a night performing, two monologues each. Out of those 170 actors they picked the best 10. Those 10 got to showcase their stuff for three weeks. I went down to the audition and I signed up. I got to come in and do a one-minute monologue. I did Matt from the *Fantasticks*. I walked in, I was number 840. I did about a third of a monologue, they said, "Thank you." I left. This was my second audition in New York. I come back the next day to see if I made one of the 170 actors. Not only was my name not on the list of 170 actors, but they had a backup list of 250; in case . . . some of those 170 dropped out or couldn't make it, they would call from that backup list. I wasn't even on the backup list. So I was quite dispirited. This weird thing happened. There were people sitting at the audition who were casting for something else that was on at this theater called the Directors Festival. This guy called me up and said, "I saw your audition; would you want to be in this play, would you want to audition for me for *The Dumbwaiter*?" I said great. I went down, auditioned, and I got it. So now I am working on this little one-act play, envious as hell of all these other actors who are showcasing their wares. So I say to the artistic director [of the Actors Fest], "If you see my work in *The Dumbwaiter* and you like it and there is an opening slot for one of those 170 guys, maybe you'll use me?" Sure enough, he did see our performance of *The Dumbwaiter*. Somebody dropped out of the twelfth night and he said, would you want to fill in? I said great. So I prepared something from *The Caretaker* and something from *Pavlo Hummel*. I put together twenty minutes and I went on stage and I did it. Then at the end of the seventeen nights they picked the best ten and guess who was picked? Moi! Now I was showcasing it and when the *New York Times* review came out, it picked me as the best of the ten. I didn't even get into the 250 backup list, but when it finally came push come to shove, I was one of the best. Because I showed up. If I hadn't shown up, that never would have happened. This artistic director went on to direct a play called *Modigliani* four years later, which he cast me in, which kind of helped me move on. You gotta show up. You never know who the hell is going to be out there.

Jack Kehler: After five years I said to myself, OK, I like this. I think that I could do this. I said, I think I can make a living at this in about ten to twelve years. Eleven years into it, I got my first movie. It was all so new and challenging and ongoing. I was learning the whole time. I really didn't have a time limit for myself. I just accepted the time between the now and the ten to twelve years. I was completely active during the whole time, being in class—continually auditioned for pieces. I was working as a waiter. I had a good community that I was a part of that I appreciated. It was something that I knew that I had to do. It was what I had to do. For me at the time it was the best thing that I could be doing. I didn't expect more things than I was having in front of me.

CHAPTER FOUR

Audition Know-How

Learning how to audition successfully is the next building block an actor must add to her tool chest of acting skills. Being able to walk onto a stage or enter a room full of strangers and audition on cue while remaining true to yourself, performing what you have prepared and staying in the moment, is a craft unto itself. It is accomplished through experience that is never exact and always depends upon the material, where you are the day of the audition, and what you believe is at stake for your career and financial situation. A reliable audition process is a fundamental requirement for every actor. When I am conducting seminars on this topic or teaching this in acting class, I pose the following question: What is the goal of an audition? Though I hear many acceptable responses, there is truly only one answer. The goal is to get the job!

But knowing that result then becomes part of the problem and not the solution. When an actor goes into audition carrying the weight of wanting a job or needing a job or fantasizing about fame and fortune, he has put himself at a disadvantage. The key to achieving your goal of getting a job is to learn *how to care less about caring*. What does this mean? An actor has to give up all the baggage that comes with an audition. Wanting to do well. Showing them you know how to act. Needing the job. By letting go of the results, you give yourself the opportunity to remain in the moment. By not concerning yourself with caring about the result, you are then able to go in there and do your work, something every actor wants to do. You may have first discovered this unknowingly for yourself when you were running late for an audition and breathlessly entered the room just happy you made it there before everyone left. Or maybe you were feeling sick and were so concerned about your health that you just wanted to audition and go home and get back into bed. The common thread here is that you were not placing any other responsibility onto the situation other than doing your job! You let go of the result and surprisingly ended up booking the part. This Zenlike state of being, staying in the moment and learning how to care less about caring, is a skill that needs to be practiced for each audition. Sometimes I quietly close my eyes, reminding myself that my concentration needs to remain focused on what I am there to do. Other times I have to do battle out loud with myself because the other considerations are taking too strong a hold on me. I remind myself that if I am to be hired for this job, they will have to see me perform the role. For me to realize the role, I must let go of the result and stay in the moment. It is the only thing that I will have control over in the audition process. When I leave the room I take a moment to evaluate how it went. I ask myself, Did I accomplish what I set out to do? Was I spontaneous when I was playing off the reader? These things occur only when I am committed to *caring less about caring*.

In preparing for an audition, an actor's responsibility is to use her craft to understand what is going on in the scene. The stronger the choice and the deeper the commitment to it, the more interesting you are as an actor. So much of auditioning is bringing yourself to the material and personalizing yourself in the conflict (comedy or drama) of the scene. That is why I have to reiterate the importance of knowing your instrument and having the craft to be able to access it on demand. For some auditions it is wise to read through the material with another actor or rehearse with a qualified audition coach. Leave yourself open to the possibility that how you first envisioned the material may change as you rehearse. Know the dialogue of the scene as well as possible. It is not a test of memorization, but a desire on your part to be off book so you can live off the reader. Being prepared is part of the process of discovery for every actor. The more you are informed about the material, the character, the relationships, and the event of the scene, the wiser you are in making decisions on how to solve it.

On the way to the audition, try to remain centered. Make sure that you are consciously breathing regularly and deeply. Shortness of breath and tension feed nervousness. By continuing to breathe and releasing the tension in your body, you'll be able to remain focused on the choices you have made. Be gentle and accepting with yourself about any anxiety that occurs within you. Know that a heightened heart rate is understandable and something every actor goes through. Remind yourself that you are not going in for brain surgery, and your life is not on the line. It is an audition. The more you audition, the better able you will be to keep the audition process in perspective. If the nervousness does not go away, then be willing to accept it, learn how to make friends with it, and if need be, use it in your work. Use your sense of humor to make light of how silly it all seems, but never beat yourself up about it. See it as your challenge in your mythical heroic journey of being an actor.

When you arrive at the audition, you first must sign in. Then find a place to sit so you can remain focused on the task at hand. You want to stay within yourself, and socializing with colleagues tends to filter that away. Don't waste your energy by comparing yourself with the other actors in the room. You may see some faces that have more professional credits than you do. There may be other actors there who don't look anything like you. A casting director wants many options for the director to choose from. Your focus needs to remain on yourself and what you are about to do. Many an audition is lost because the actor loses concentration in the waiting room. While waiting quietly for your turn, check to make sure you are breathing. Do your best to let go of whatever physical tension you are holding on to. If need be, recite your script to yourself, be clear about your intention in the scene, or inwardly say a prayer that can give you the strength to share your gift. When your name is called, take another moment to breathe. Depending on what you are reading for, there may be one or several people in the room when you are auditioning. Know for yourself you are entering as the problem solver. They need to cast an actor, and hopefully if you look the part and can act, you will be their answer. With that in mind, I like to bring my good social skills with me into the room and acknowledge everyone who is there. In the meantime I am juggling my inner concentration as I am about to audition. Trust your instincts in this situation as to whether or not you should make any conversation with those in attendance. As you develop these audition skills, you'll know what works best for you.

Take a breath once you are about to start and commit to your choice as fully as possible. In certain situations some casting directors will read the other part with you or will have hired a reader. Whatever preparations you have made regarding the scene, it is imperative that you now begin to live off the person that you are reading with by being in the *now*. Make sure you are communicating to and listening to the reader. Allow for spontaneity by not adhering rigidly to any preconceived notions. Whether the other person is reading well or not, use what is going on between the two of you during the audition. It is your responsibility to connect with her in the scene. If the audition is not going well, you'll have to make an instant judgment to decide if it would it be in your best interest to stop and start again. This is absolutely acceptable. Politely ask to start over, but do not make any excuses for your work. You are being hired to have grace under pressure, so take a breath and say where you want to start and begin again. As an actor you must realize this is your time and the more you can use what is going on for you in the room at that moment, the better off you will be. When the audition is over, take a moment for yourself. Some actors will ask the director if he would like them to do the scene another way. Use your sense of what is going on in the room to determine if that might be useful for you. If there is nothing else to say, thank them for the opportunity, wish them good luck, and walk out with your head held high. If the audition went well, enjoy it. If the audition went poorly, learn from it. What could you have done differently? Did you do what you set out to do, and why or why not? Spend whatever time you need to process the experience; then move on. Don't linger or beat yourself over the head about it. Remember it is an audition and the sooner you move on to the next one, the better off you will be. Know for yourself that as a working actor, you will spend more time auditioning than actually working.

As I have previously mentioned in this chapter, the point of auditioning is to get the job, first and foremost. However, there are ancillary benefits in the audition process that need to be mentioned. You want to leave a favorable impression on the casting director, for she is the one who is the go-between for you and the director. Though you may not be cast in the role you just read for, she may recognize your talent and call you in for another project down the line. For episodic television, feature films, and theater companies, your greatest ally is the casting director, who knows your work and can champion you when a casting decision is being made. Much casting is done according to type and how you match up to the other actors. A director or producer unable to use you in the role he has just seen you audition for may have another project in the future that you may be better suited for. For some television shows, you just have to keep going back multiple times before your number is chosen.

It is important to know that the more you audition, the better you will become at it. You will develop more confidence within yourself and you will become friendlier with the audition process. As an auditioning exercise, look to audition for a play in an out-of-the-way theater for something you may or may not be really interested in doing. Still prepare, but discover what it is like to audition when there is nothing at stake for you. That sense of freedom from result, while acting for the sake of acting, is what you want to feel when auditioning when there is money on the line. As actors we will always have questions about how we are working because we are inquisitive, creative souls. It's out of our hands whether we are chosen for the role. What we are in charge of is leaving a lasting impression on those who are in that room. We plant the seeds for future opportunities. You never know when the door will open for you, but you must keep knocking to be heard.

Carol Potter: The fear of not being seen, of not being valued, of not being understood, not being gotten was just paralyzing for me. I had to work incredibly hard to develop my audition process. So that I could go into an audition and feel *that I did what I wanted to do*. In the beginning it was all too often strangled by my fear. It made me very tight, it made me very emotionally unresponsive to the material. It inhibited me. Like the worst thing that you can possibly be as an actor. That was a tremendous challenge. It took me a long time to come to the recognition that when I walked into a room, if I started comparing myself favorably to the other people in the room, that was just a step towards comparing myself unfavorably to the other people in the room. The only way I was going to get beyond this was to separate myself from any kind of comparison whatsoever, and focus simply on my own process. You have to come to a Zen place—of putting myself on the line and giving them everything I had and recognizing that might not get me the job. That they are unrelated issues. It was very, very difficult to separate those two. Especially in the beginning of one's career, there is the truth that there are probably things that you can do better. So you want to be open to the feedback that you can get. But it also can be very wrenching and difficult. You also have to know that this is an issue that, I have to stand on my own and do what feels right.

Brent Jennings: One of the problems with auditions is a lot of times we go in an audition and it's just another audition. It's just an episodic TV thing or it's a role you really don't care about in a film. It's easy to develop bad audition habits when you audition for things that you don't really care about. . . . When it's an ideal situation, I try to approach it like, this is my opportunity to perform this role. And it's a performance. I'm going to do the role right now. I'm not auditioning, I'm going in doing the role. I prepare for it as if it's a performance. As if it's opening night for a Broadway play. I try to spend as much time with the material as possible. I like to get it as much time ahead [as possible] if it's something I want. If I'm really hot on it. I don't want the material a day or two before the audition. I want a week with it. I want to go over it, I want to think about it. If there's any research, if it's based on some stories, based on a book, I want to read the book. All those things that you get excited about [it], that you can do to fuel your creativity, is what you should do. You should look at it as your opportunity to go in and give your performance. Your interpretation, your take on that role. It's your time. You go in there and there is nobody else that exists in the room but you. None of the other actors waiting to go in exist. Whatever time you need and you go in and it's yours. You own it for that amount of time. They buy it or they lease it or they reject it or whatever.

Ethan Phillips: For auditions I acknowledge that I'm fearful, I acknowledge that I'm nervous. I do this process that works for me where I make friends with it. I look at it like if it wasn't for these nerves, I wouldn't be able to do this. I look at the nerves as the fuel that keeps me charged and in touch with myself. It means I care and this matters to me. That's all positive stuff and I try to make that work. When I go in I take a big breath and I'm prepared. They can shove anything at me at an audition and I can make an adjustment. I've made my choices and I then try to throw it away. But I don't hang on to my choices like they're precious jewels. Even though I'm nervous as hell, the form is there. Hopefully I can even surprise myself.

Christine Estabrook: Actually drama school is no training for working in the profession, unless you are going into the rep [repertory] companies. Auditioning is a whole different thing. It has really nothing to do with all your training as an actor. You kind of train yourself to work with your own instrument in an audition. The work that you do at home on the audition is just to get a handle on the role. I've learned through many years not to be intimidated by the audition. To go in and do the role the way I want to do it. I did have a period of time where I did try and give them what they did want to see and that was successful too. Where I am in my career now, I do what I want to do with the role. If I succeed in doing that, then I feel as though I've had a successful audition even though I don't get the part or if I do get the part. It's hard to go in front of a group of people because you take [it] personally, you can tell if you're a sensitive actor, you can tell if they are with you or if they have already cast the part. You can just tell. Some audition rooms have an attitude about you as soon as you walk through the door, just by what you look like. Try not to let that get in your way. Try to be polite and pleasant, try to be yourself. It's hard when they are not giving you [anything]—some give, some don't. The worst is going to the network because that is all about their karma with each other. The people who are fighting with each other in the room about who they want for the part. It's like stand-up. You try to do your act and not be aggressive or negative towards the people, whatever they are giving you. You play to the people who are laughing. [*laughs*]

Kevin Bourland: I think I was having more fun in the [commercial] audition process. I didn't take it as seriously, so I came across better. I found I was better in those tighter moments. It came easier for me. I think part of it was just natural. I also figured out how to get the jobs, what they were looking for. You walk into the room, you only have a few moments in a commercial. It was reading the room, reading the people. It was always something I had innately. I am able to read people and get a negative or positive vibe. I was bolder. I would tell them if I did a take in an audition, I would tell them, I want to do it again. I had a lot more balls auditioning commercially. I learned right away when I started directing [commercials that] I had no idea how little the ad agency people and the client—how little they think of actors. That was the first thing I found out when I went onto the other side during the casting process. What I look for [when casting] are people that are just honest, not on. They can screw up and not panic—just themselves. Of course a commercial is really a lot about type. How people talk to each other and how they talk to the camera. That will get them a callback.

Robin Bartlett: What I believe is whatever you're feeling at the moment is going to show. Trying to manipulate yourself into feeling something different is not going to work. If you're nervous or if you're tired—whatever you bring with you—that is what is there. At least present that honestly. To me the easiest way to do that is to know what I am about to say and then let it happen. That really is my technique. I learned part of that from Michael Moriarity, who I worked with. If you bring with you just the state that you are in and the pleasure that you take in acting, that is all you really need. If you can hook into that each time—I combine that with something I learned from Woody Allen. The first thing he said to me was, "Forget the lines." I forgot the lines and I panicked. Then I noticed that this was brilliant advice. If you know the lines you can forget them, and then they will occur to you in the same way that spontaneous speech occurs to you.

Hal Landon: If you are trying to list the worst possible conditions under which to act, the audition situation meets all of them. [*laughs*] No time to prepare. The people watching you are not trying to share the performance with you, they are judging what you are doing. You're not performing with other actors. There's no reality in terms of the environment. It's kind of madness really. But it is also an interesting challenge. When I started to think of that in those terms, I started to do better. What I would sometimes do is the characterization—which you can do more of on stage—the transformation of you to whoever the character is can be a pretty broad leap. It is much harder to do that in film and television. Especially auditioning for film and television. Most of this comes from audition experiences. Finally one casting director told me when you audition [for these people], they have taste and talent but they don't know much about acting. When someone comes as themselves and becomes somebody else, they go, "Oh, now he's acting. We don't want acting, we want believability." I suppose once you are bankable, like a Dustin Hoffman, Daniel Day Lewis, and make that transformation, those people go, "That man is a chameleon, he can do anything." It is pretty hard for us to come in and do that.

Barry Shabaka Henley: I heard John Cusack being interviewed on *Fresh Air* by Terry Gross, and he was talking about being a lousy auditioner. I thought, wow, that's good to hear. I'm not out here alone. They said,

"What have you done to compensate for that?" He said, "I really learn the material." I thought that is so simple. I wouldn't learn the material! Now the difference is the kind of preparation I do. I prepare as if they are going to shoot. I do it like I got one take in that office and they are going to shoot it. What they do in the office is going on the air. I have to prepare myself as if I'm going into a performance. I still don't like it at all. It's nerve-racking. I've learned a skill that has allowed me to work myself through it.

Amy Aquino: I read the material and I see what hits me. I rarely read it over and over. I'm not somebody who reads the script three times. I see what in the character hits me. I always make a little chitchat. Some people say you shouldn't—just walk into the room and do your own thing. I tend to chat with people and break the ice. Before I go into my audition I make sure I give myself the time I need to collect myself. Figure out where I am, what I need to place before the scene. Get familiar with the material but not off book—I always carry the page. Then try to surprise them—that's always what I do when I look at the material. You can always read what's there and put some emotion to it, but I always try to surprise them a little bit. I almost always try to find some humor no matter what. If the room is dead, if they're terrified and they don't know how to react, I can't help them and bring them out of that. I don't end up beating myself about very much about auditions.

Lucinda Jenney: You have to know the medium you are auditioning for. Television, they like you to know the words, they don't like you to change things around. They want you to give them within the scope of what they want. Film, oftentimes you are working one-to-one with a director and he has a vision. But he also wants you to help him with that vision. So you have a little more freedom to say, "This doesn't work for me. Can I try this?" It becomes a personal rapport that comes through experience. Television is more cut-and-dry. They want to know you can do the job in a certain amount of time and not give them too much trouble. However, everybody wants the part illuminated.

James Rebhorn: I look at it as a little miniperformance. I am there to solve their problem. I do think they are as uncomfortable, feel as awkward and as up in the air about this situation, and are nervous about it as I am. They do have a problem—they have to cast this role. Figure out who this character is. I look at the audition as an opportunity to help solve their problem. The way that I do that is by making strong choices, by preparing it, by making it like a little performance. Then I like to give them—the director—an opportunity to work with me. I try to end my audition after I do the scene and say, "Would you like me to do that again? Is there anything you'd like to try differently?" I like to give them opportunity to work with me. To see if we can actually work together in a very condensed, unpressured atmosphere. Finally after I get through it once, a lot of the pressure is off. For all of us.

Anne DeSalvo: When I was younger I used to go in thinking I had to go in as the character. Now I go in as me; then I go into the character. I very often ask them a question, which engages them and starts a rap-port—a connection—it makes you more special than just coming in and plopping into the chair. It's like, "Oh, she's interesting—remember that girl who came in?" I think it's a good idea to create a rapport when you go in. Don't go into an audition thinking that these people are going to reject you, they are going to harm you, hurt you. You're going into a room of people who really want to find someone great in this part. And I am great for this part. This is a wonderful opportunity for me to share my talent. Nobody knows what makes things work and everybody is looking over their shoulder—that's why there is so much insecurity—my feeling is be as confident as you possibly can. If there are people in the room that are unsure and you walk in sure, it's like, "Hey, let's go with that one."

Clyde Kusatsu: What has happened now after thirty-one years is I approach the audition process differently. Before I had this cocky confidence and I would wing it in there and let my personality do it. Now I go over the material to become familiar with it—not use any tricks—but the best is to get it from the heart. Before I would go, "I'm dying, this is not happening." I wouldn't stop, I'd keep on going and I'd sink deeper and deeper and it would be terrible. Now I'd go, "I'm sorry, could I stop? Let me go back; it's not there." I take a break and get myself centered. Not being afraid to fall on your face, admit it in their presence, and start over again.

Nike Doukas: I think young actors will find that you get the material [tel-evision or film] and if you're used to doing theater, you get the material and you feel uninspired by it. You don't even know how to wrap your mouth around the words, it's so uninteresting. I am finally getting to the point where I can find something interesting about every piece of paper I can pick up. That is your job, to find something interesting that you have to bring to it. Not to worry about what you think they want because ultimately it is like going on a date. If you have good chemistry, they are going to ask you out, and if you don't, they're not. You can't control that. You have to bring what makes you special and believe in that. Find what is happening in my life right now that I can relate to in this material and get excited about it. Get off book and give the performance you are going to give on camera. At the same time, be willing to take direction and be brave enough to make a mistake. You have to keep loose and free, and they recognize that too. They want to see something spontaneous and alive. It takes *a lot* of practice.

Robert Picardo: I have talked to so many wonderful actors who say they can't audition, they hate auditioning, or sometimes they have great auditions or they have lousy auditions. You think that an actor gets to a certain stage in his career where they have done enough work, that they would go in and have at least a very professional, impressive audition, no matter what they are auditioning for. It doesn't seem to be the case. If you audition your whole life, you go through periods where you are auditioning great and you can't seem to make a mistake. Then you go through periods when you're not auditioning great. Do I know the how and why of that? No, I don't have an answer for that. I do know when I audition the most successfully—I walk in the door with the attitude that I am a problem solver and a collaborator. I understand that they have a problem, which is they have to find someone to play this role. Let me see what I can contribute. When I take that tack— when it's all about how do we fix this rather than let me show you how great I am, [*laughs*] let me show you how deeply I feel, how loud I can scream. It's really about let me work with you to solve this problem. That's when I do my best work. I tell myself that all the time and there are just as many times when I go in and you'd never know I had that philosophy.

April Grace: A director once said to me, never think of this as an audition. You are not auditioning, you are coming here to be this person. That helped tremendously. The difference in my mindset between going in and doing a show because you've got the gig and going in to audition for the show is completely different. I spend a lot of time now in my own mind walking in as if I already have the gig. This is not an audition, I'm coming here to show you what you are going to be putting on tape. That has been incredibly helpful. In television what they see in the audition room, they want to see that when they get in there [on the set]. It is not the same process as the theater, where the characterization grows and grows. They want you to walk and be it—they don't want to think about it. Unless you are the lead, but we are not talking about the movie star people. Don't forget this is your time. These people are there to see you because you're fantastic at what you do. You have a story they need to hear; take your time and tell that story. Don't let them rush you.

Armin Shimerman: I had such butterflies at TV auditions, film auditions, that I know I shot myself in the foot constantly. Invariably I would fuck up. I'd stumble over words, I begged to read it again, I'd make inane conversation when I was in there. I was just so terrified of the audition process because every time I auditioned, nothing happened. One of the things I learned eventually was to say fuck it. What's the worst thing that can happen? I don't get the job? I didn't get the last fifty auditions, so what difference does it make? Just go in and do the best you can. When I took the onus of needing to get the job, which was paramount at this time—I needed to get this work—when I slipped out from underneath that shadow, then the auditions got better.

Steve Vinovich: Going to network, I find, is one of the most frightening things on this planet. I call it the actors Olympics. You're down to one shot. You've got your ten seconds. "Don't fuck up" hanging over you like a vengeance. It's all about the money. Ahh! When you first get the audition you go in and you are loose and do the audition and have fun and, great, they like you. They call you back. Then you come back in, now the director is there, maybe a producer. You do it again, OK. Then you get a third callback, maybe a fourth callback, where they've got more people, more and more giving you more. And now they are preparing you for network. Before you go into network you have to make a deal with the networks. They won't let you go in without making a deal. So now we are talking, you know, thirty thousand dollars a week and you're adding it up, twenty-six shows, thirty thousand. God, I can't even count that high! Multiply. And you have eight lines in the scene, maybe, now each line is worth approximately ninety-four thousand dollars. Then when you get there, you sign your papers with your ninety-four thousand. Now you're buying the car, the home, the pools, you've got the kids out there in the orchard. It's every dream come true as you go in and you're going to audition for network with your eight lines. So now your heart is pounding, you're trying to breathe deep. Other guys are standing around, your competition. You go into a tiny little office, usually with about eighty thousand people in it. And you have about a foot of space to work in and you do your eight lines. Sometimes you do them great and you get it. Sometimes you do them great and you don't get it. Sometimes you die a slow, lingering death [*laughs*] where you know you're dying. I died a big one. I had one like this. I went in, it was just another show as far as I knew, but it was my sixth time back. As I went in the writer-producer says, "You're our first choice, don't blow it." Then they kept me waiting for two hours before I went in. By [the] time I went in I was gone. I was a wreck. So I thought I'd look at the star, he was going to read with me, I'd concentrate on him, that would help me. I looked at him and his eyes were bigger than mine, he was terrified. He was terrified. I just stunk up the joint, you know. I knew I'd blown it. I just choked. It turned out that show was *Seinfeld*. [The role was Kramer.] I ran into Larry David [the creator] later, "Weren't you the guy who was going to be . . . ?" I said, "Yeah, yeah." He said, "I'm sorry. We did rather well." [*laughs*] So you never know, you never know.

CHAPTER FIVE

Life on the Set

Your telephone rings and you anxiously answer it and say, "Hello." It's your agent. Your heart skips a beat, as you have been praying to hear good news. "You booked the job. Congratulations." It is an exciting moment of accomplishment and affirmation. After years of study and countless auditions, you are going to get paid to act. There is a sense of relief in knowing where your next paycheck will be coming from. After hearing numerous times they liked you but they decided to go another way, or they made an offer to someone else, it is a great feeling to know that this time *you* were chosen to play the role.

Depending on the type of job, the next person to call you will usually be someone from the wardrobe department, to check for correct sizes and set up a wardrobe fitting. In commercials you get paid a modest fee to go in to be fitted (film and television fittings don't pay), so make sure you sign a time sheet when you arrive at the production company. The next phone call you receive will be from a second assistant director (second AD) or a production assistant (PA), who will give you a call time and location map—when and where to report. If a script is to be sent to your home, they'll check to make sure they have a current address so it may be delivered properly. The envelope will contain a script, sometimes with multiple-colored pages for each rewritten version, and a call sheet with everyone's name, contact number, and job assignment for the project. For film and one-hour television, there may also be a one-line schedule. That comes from the production office and states the shooting schedule and which scenes are to be shot for each day of filming. This is always subject to change. The call sheet will also have each actor listed with a number beside his or her name. Look for your name and number and reference the call sheet to know which scenes you are in, which actor(s) you will be working with, and when you will be shooting. Actors need to be flexible: the scene you auditioned for may have changed dramatically. That has nothing to do with you. The script needed alteration because of time or the need of the star's character to accomplish something that was not foreseen in the original.

I have acted in commercials, industrial films, soap operas, hour and half-hour television, and motion pictures. Here is what I do to make working an enjoyable and successful process: I come with a positive attitude. I am grateful for having the opportunity to act and getting paid for doing so. I look to get along with everyone. I treat all members of the crew with respect because they are an integral part of the filmmaking process. I don't call unwarranted attention to myself. From long experience, I know that I will be recognized and appreciated for the work that I do. The more friendly and cooperative you are, and the more prepared you are to act your role, the more pleasant and productive your day will be. I also bring something to read or a project to work on, to keep myself busy during the endless downtime that comes with acting on film. An actor I know practices his saxophone in his dressing room, another paints, and some have taken up crocheting.

When you first report to the set you meet with a second AD, who will take you to your dressing room or trailer and hand you contracts to sign. At the end of the day when you sign out, ask to receive your copy of the contracts. Remember you are an independent contractor. Take the responsibility to keep track of your time so if there are any disputes later on, you have a record of your day's work. Next you are sent to hair and makeup. When I am sitting in the makeup chair, I tend to focus my conversation away from show business. I enjoy having the makeup artist or hairstylist tell me about herself and how she is holding up working on the set. If you like your hair or makeup styled in a certain fashion, mention it to the stylist. I stay away from gossip and show my appreciation for how I look after the stylist has completed his job. Some actors will study their lines while in the chair, get some needed rest, or read a magazine. Actors tend to form a bond with this department because of the personal interaction that naturally occurs, and therefore it is important to be friendly with everyone there.

The format for shooting film or one-hour television is quite different from that for shooting half-hour situation comedies. Film or one-hour television is shot nonsequentially while sitcoms and soap operas are shot in sequence, as if you were doing a play. Film or one-hour television may shoot a master shot with a single camera before going in for close-ups and two-shots (when two characters are in frame). Half-hour TV shows or soaps are multiple-camera shows with as many as four cameras shooting simultaneously. By using this many cameras at the same time, they are in a position to capture all the action (master, close-ups, two-shots) while a scene is being filmed.

Half-hour television begins with a table reading and is on a five-day shooting schedule. The table reading is an opportunity for the script to be heard by the writers and producers. Next they work on the script and then send new pages in a different color to the actors for the following day's rehearsal. Half-hour shows or soap operas are shot on a large sound stage. There is an established operating set already in place. If a new episode requires an additional setting, it will be built for that week's show. The director stages a scene for the actors to walk through and for the camera operators to watch so they know where they will place the cameras. Other department heads and sound and lights will also watch so they will know where they will set up their equipment when it comes time to shoot. Each scene will travel on the same stage from one established set to another, with the actors, director, and department heads moving with you. As the week continues, the actors are challenged by the constant revisions in the script. It is wise not to memorize your part until late in the week because there are always changes. During the week there will be a run-through for the network executives and all the writers and producers. Be aware that you are constantly working because you never know when someone, like a producer or a studio representative, may make a comment about your acting. On the fifth day there will be a dress rehearsal and then a performance in front of a studio audience. Nowadays after the performance, the creative staff of a show will determine where pickups (filming midpoint in a scene) are necessary. They will shoot late into the night without an audience to get additional camera coverage, change some dialogue, or rework a gag they felt was missed in the earlier performances. A few half-hour comedies are now shot single-camera-style on film without a laugh track and audience, similar to hour-long episodic television. Actors need to come to work ready to adapt to the constant changes in the script and the timing and energy that is needed in situation comedies.

Soap operas shoot similarly to half-hour television, but they do it on a daily basis without an audience. A soap opera actor spends much of her time memorizing the script beforehand. When you report to work you will have a quick walk-through of a scene, perhaps in a rehearsal room, with the director, and then you will move onto to the set to shoot. You'll notice that soaps have little character behavior compared with film, and actors can end up living on the words. Experienced actors on soaps are able to infuse their character with a strong inner life beyond just saying the words. Soaps have historically been opportunities for young actors to break into the business and for mature veterans to continue to perform on television while seeking work on stage and film.

Hour television and film can require very long days depending on your call time, shooting schedule, and how many scenes and the length of the scenes you are involved in. When you are on the set you can end up sitting in your dressing room for long periods of time. Patience is essential. You will not be forgotten. When it is your time to report to the set a production assistant will come and get you. In your dressing room you will receive your *sides*. This is a miniaturized printed version of the scenes in the script that will be filmed that day. When you arrive on the set, you will be greeted by the first assistant director. Hopefully he will introduce you to the other cast members and the director. On a film, which you may have been cast for several weeks or months earlier, the director may not remember who you are. I make it my business to introduce myself if no one comes over to say hello. The director and the first assistant director will then place you on the set and have all the actors, with sides in hand, run through the dialogue. This is an opportunity for the director to hear the words and make sure the action in the scene is how he envisioned it. If you have any questions about the script or story line, now is a good time to ask. After a second run-through, the different film department heads will come in to watch so they will know how to set up their crews when filming begins. These run-throughs are for the most part quite perfunctory for the actors, and whatever emotional life the scene requires should be held off until the actual filming takes place. As the crews then set up to film, you are on break from the set. During this period you are free to go to craft services for a snack or drink. You may want to go back to your dressing room, run your lines, or do whatever you need to do to be ready to work.

In hour television and film, the director will usually shoot a master shot that includes all the actors and extras that are in the scene from start to finish. This is an establishing shot that is wide enough to encapsulate the entire action of the scene with all the actors. As an actor you must pace yourself so as not to empty the well, so to speak, in the master. It is when the director moves the camera in for single-or two-shot close-ups that you want to begin to bring to the surface the emotional life of the character. Depending upon the director, time restraints, and your ability to deliver the goods when called upon, you will do take after take after take after take, until the director has captured the scene to his satisfaction. This is where pacing yourself becomes absolutely vital. In film, the camera then needs to be repositioned so as to shoot the reverse of the shot just taken to capture any dialogue not heard and action not seen. This requires another setup with all the departments and another waiting period for the actor. On certain sets there may be another two cameras rolling simultaneously, known as the B and C cameras. When you are performing off camera (you will be placed next to the camera at the correct eye line, enabling the on-camera actor to have someone to act with), it is your job to be available for the actors who are being filmed. Keep your performance alive so your colleagues have something they can live off. A well-respected actor is someone who continues to act off camera as well as on. The repetition of acting throughout the day in film can be an exhausting process, so it is essential to maintain energy and focus.

The major difference in shooting between hour episodic television and motion pictures is that in an eight-day shooting schedule for episodic television, shooting multiple scenes in one day happens rapidly. Motion pictures offer more time for the director and actors to make discoveries while they work. A movie director may also have had lengthy conversations with the cast about characters and relationships that a television director just doesn't have the time for. Some film directors will set up rehearsal time for the actors to rehearse and work on the scenes without the pressure of being filmed. Actors in movies also have more time to do the necessary research into who their characters are, to create their behavior, and to understand what motivates them. Needless to say, acting in a film may be a more creative and improvisational acting experience. Television is more of a writer-producer medium. In both film and television, there is a script supervisor. Her job is to check for shooting continuity (an actor must repeat physical behavior that matches previous takes) in the script as well as to make sure the actors are reciting the correct dialogue.

All actors will flub a line at one time or another and the script supervisor is there to help when needed. In film an unscripted spontaneous moment may end up in the final edit, but some television shows are dialogue-exact.

Acting in commercials is similar to acting in film in terms of how the shooting takes place. When I first started acting in commercials, I envisioned it as an opportunity to be the lead actor in a thirty-second film. The greatest difference is that the product is the star. Some commercials are a slice of life where there is a truthful interaction taking place between actors. Other types of commercials may involve a spokesperson pitching a product or actors demonstrating the merchandise. Another added dimension to acting in commercials is that you get feedback not only from the director but also from an advertising agency producer, who will confer with the client, who is on the set as well. They will approach a director with their concerns about your performance. I always find it best to seek direction from only one person, and that is the director.

Working in commercials has given me the opportunity to travel and work with award-winning directors and directors of photography. Most importantly, all actors realize that with commercials come residuals. (In film there are residuals for video and DVD sales as well as when a movie appears on pay or free TV. Episodic and half-hour television has residual payment for reruns.) Principal work for a day on a commercial currently pays $530, but the residuals can lead into the thousands. Commercials can then become a means to an end in supporting yourself while you continue to seek legitimate theatrical work. Years ago many actors looked down on commercials and thought they were too good to act in them. Over the years that has changed dramatically with movie and television stars acting in commercials around the world. When I was a young actor in New York, I worked as an extra in commercials. In the background, I learned from watching the principals perform, experienced what it was like to be on a set, and was fortunate to be upgraded a few times and become eligible for residuals. I never thought of myself as an extra, but as an actor getting started. As a working actor, I look to earn my living by balancing a career between commercials, television, film, and stage. Union work through SAG and AFTRA creates residuals, puts money in my pension plan, and affords me health benefits.

Many well-respected working actors supplement their living as voice-over artists in commercials for radio and television and in cartoons. This can be a very lucrative career for an actor who has a unique sound or a pliable voice for creating different types of characters. A voice-over artist has a unique opportunity to perform a role that goes unseen by an audience but is communicated through her voice. If you are the type of actor who can "speak the speech I pray you trippingly on the tongue," and has an improvisatory gift with speech, this is an excellent venue to pursue. Most commercial agencies have a voice-over department. As in all areas of show business, it is a highly competitive field and there are opportunities to study with qualified voice coaches. Another voice-related career for a working actor to pursue is joining a *loop group*. Looping is done in postproduction on film and television to add voices to the background players in a scene that needs to be filled in. Loopers will stand individually or in a group, in front of a microphone in an additional dialogue recording (ADR) studio, and create conversations for the extras, who were mouthing the words while the actual filming took place. This too is an excellent source of revenue for a working actor, as there are residuals for looping. Any actor who loves improv and has an interesting sound should look into the field of voice work.

❖ ❖ ❖ ❖

Marianne Muellerleile: With a guest star you're coming into an established family unit. You are only there five days—if you're lucky. You could be there [only] three, two, or one. You're never going to be on the inside of that family, so don't fight it. Enjoy that you have the job. My emphasis is always to concentrate on the work and not what star is on the show or to become somebody's best friend. Or [that] this somehow is going to lead to something—that's all ridiculous. Don't even bother. You be the best you can be. You be the most professional, you be the first there. Never be late. I think it's important to remember when you're a guest star, you're a temp, a temp worker. It is a business. I don't need to make a buddy. I don't need to make somebody love me. I need to be the best I can be at that job. Be the most professional. Be pleasant. Don't gossip. That stuff can only bring you down the [wrong] road. There are so many people on a set who are watching you, who know you are there, have made a decision about your talent, about bringing you into this family. You never know, the second assistant to the casting director, who five years from now can be the head of casting at Paramount. There are one hundred people on a set who are going to know who you are that you will never know. My motto is to have a smooth, easy, upbeat, happy-to-be-employed, good-at-the-job kind of week and go for the next one.

Shelley Morrison: Think fast on your feet. Be very, very open. Know that they will be changing lines constantly. On tape night we do the first pass on a scene; then the writers and the producers get into a huddle and rewrite the whole scene. They'll call you over to the script supervisor's little desk and they'll say, "Shelley, say this, don't say this. Megan, say this, don't say this. Sean, say this, don't say this. OK, just run it. Do it." Second scene, the same thing. You have to be agile. We've had big-name guest stars run screaming into the night not being able to work so quickly. Know that from the table read to the tape night, it's not going to be the same script. You may have three, four, five scenes in the table read and you'll be down to two lines by the time we tape. It has nothing to do with your ability. It all has to do with the pace of the show, the timing of the show. In rehearsal sometimes they see the story leading one way and the other story isn't working, so they have to change the B story. I advise young people to come to tapings of a sitcom and see how people work.

Lauren Tom: In musical comedy you have to learn the timing and have the comedy chops. There is a certain rhythm you have to learn. Being a dancer helped me feel that rhythm [in sitcoms]—when someone throws you the line, you come back with the punch line. It is almost something you have to feel innately. It's like being a baseball player—I need to hit it right there [*snaps her fingers*]—it's like a setup and then you've got to come up with it. Sitcom work pays astronomical salaries, but it is one of the most stressful jobs I've had. I've been a series regular on a few different series—I always love it because it is a sense of family, but it is really stressful. If the joke doesn't work they are going to give you a new one thirty seconds before you have to tape it. Often it's a live show and you're performing the show. That's what makes it like the theater also—they'll do it from beginning to end. You're putting on a show for the live audience.

Nestor Carbonell: The way I see it, there isn't any half-hour training, maybe workshops. I generally don't believe in that stuff. Good half-hour acting is rooted in truth. If it is not truthful, it is not funny. The situation has to be funny in and of itself. For you to start hamming it up is generally not funny. It has got to be grounded in truth. It is a little bit of heightened energy, but only in the sense of a bit of stage energy. You're not performing to an audience even though there is almost always an audience of three or four hundred people. You can't play to them because there are four cameras on you. While you're allowing them in, you're doing film work really. When people first try it out they feel they are playing to this studio audience. It's something you learn really quickly— you've got to bring it down, it's really to [the] camera. You allow the audience to give you energy. You feed off their energy. For me there is a bit of science to it, a bit of math to it. Figuring out where the jokes are, understanding why it's funny. Understand it even intellectually, if I do have trouble with it. When you do half-hour you have to repeat that joke six times during the week in front of the network, the studio, the writers, so you hope it doesn't go stale by the time you get to an audience. If I have to work on a joke, I know why it works. Understanding the joke and learning not to tip it. And as soon as you hit the joke, get out of there. [*laughs*] Don't linger, move on and keep doing; stick to your objective. You don't want to be languishing in the laughter.

Anne-Marie Johnson: Half-hour to me is the best work going, but it's the most difficult. When you get cast in a half-hour show the decisions are made by committee. You've got a show runner [producer], eight writers, the network, and the studio. And sometimes the director [*laughs*], [though] he or she has the least to say about what you are supposed to do. Sitcom work is very difficult because you are never certain that you are going to stay on—you are easily replaced in sitcom work. At the table read when you are meeting all the actors and opening up the script, the minute you step into that room you're still auditioning. That's what I found very disconcerting, even when I was a series regular. You're always trying to represent your best; there is no time to relax. You have to have a sitcom energy, you always have to be ready to rehearse, you always have to be ready to try something new. You really have to be able to bend and go with the flow and not get to overwhelmed. When you get razzled and frazzled, they have absolutely no respect for you. To be a sitcom performer and have some longevity in it, you can't take things personally—you really have to be on your toes.

Christine Estabrook: A lot of times I play guest-star roles, you play the emotional part of the person who is breaking down, who is in crisis, so that the regular can look good by making you feel better about your idiocy or something. You are always there as a guest star to make the regulars look better. You really have to stay focused. If you walk on a set and you insist on staying focused, everyone will appreciate that. Everyone will allow that. The whole staff and everyone else really works off of what you are about. I just did an hour TV show where I was a guest. I had to walk onto the set looking at everybody's feet because I really had to stay in the space I was in. You have to turn it on and off so fast. You just get your job done much faster if you can allow yourself to do that.

Shannon Kenny: Some directors give you nothing; some will help. Some directors will give you a few adjustments, which is great acting-wise. You get little things—where to walk, where to stand—they'll tell you to bring it down or up. Sometimes if you are lucky you'll get a director who knows the through line of the episode and can help you—it's like a puzzle and you're not sure where to arc your story, where to hit the emotional points of the characters' journey. Sometimes they give you nice praise and give you some confidence and sometimes they give you nothing. You've got to learn not to want anything from them. That's a big thing—don't expect anything, in terms of praise, you won't get it. You'll get it one day and you won't the next. Just know how busy they are. They don't have time to stop and tell you you're doing a good job. Quite often once that scene is over, they are in a high-pressure situation to get the next three scenes done by the end of the day. Really know that.

Steve Vinovich: Guest starring on shows is awful. It is not much fun usually. You're rushed, they don't have much time for you. If you are doing a lawyer or doctor show, good luck because you are speaking in tongues. You don't know what the hell you are saying. You're rarely rehearsed or [you're] underrehearsed. They just want to get it shot and over with. Some have been fun, but it's a horrible situation. It's being thrown into a pit of terror. Everybody on the set is hurried and scared, it seems. Most shows you work aren't that much fun. You think they are going to be fun, but they aren't. TV is not very satisfying for your art, but it is great for your wallet.

Roxanne Hart: There are so many business elements, marketing elements—people who come in and have something to say about what your character is doing. It seems to have very little to do with the artistic impulse or the impulse to tell the story. It is about something else. The network shows have a responsibility to support a sponsor. It affects your work as an actor. If you are working on an HBO show—I was working on *Oz* and when I first took the character on, the character was one way, [then] he [writer-producer Tom Fontana] took this character out in a very wild, bizarre, and totally fabulous as an actor-artist creative journey. I don't think he would have been able to do [that] in network television. The thing that a series can do is it can give you a sense of stability. It can give you financial stability—it can give you a certain amount of name value—that can help you get in some cases those independent films that you really want to do.

Lee Garlington: I expect nothing from a director, though I am very much a director's actor. If you tell me something as a director that I think is completely wrong, I am going to give it to you 100 percent—and hope and pray that you are going to see that. If you really like what has just happened, I am going to ask you if you can give me one shot to do it the way my gut tells me to do it. In my experience theater is the playwright's medium. Television basically belongs to the producers, and film belongs to the director. Some television, depending on who the director is, belongs to the director. There are star-run sets, producer-run sets, director-run sets—they're all different.

Anne-Marie Johnson: Hour-long is very different from half-hour. There is very little decision by committee because once you start shooting, it's in the [film] can. It's too expensive to reshoot. There is very little rehearsal—I'm shocked if I ever get to rehearse for hour-long. The director is really directing you. You have so much more time to work on your character. You spend more time sitting in your dressing room than you do shooting. It's an eight-day schedule. You get to know your costars a little better. You become more of a family. The hours are longer. There is more time to relax. I was never as fearful about losing my job. If I had my druthers, although there is more fun doing a half-hour, there is much more mental security doing an hour.

Gregory Itzin: There are different kinds of behavior on the part of guest stars. I try to be as professional as possible. Be friendly, don't need friends. I try to be gracious, be nice to the people who take care of you—the hair people, the makeup people, the assistant directors, the cameraman—as much as possible get to know them. Don't treat them like the help because they can make you or break you. It is good common sense as well as good common decency. Don't try to become friends with the leads because they don't need another friend and they have people asking them for stuff right and left. If it happens you have a common ground, that's fine. If you're the guest star your needs are secondary to the going-ons of the piece. Once again, keep a low profile, do your job, know your words, show up, and do the best you can.

Aaron Lustig: Everyone knows there are very few character people on soap operas, except for the small day-player-type stuff. It is very rare to see a character guy on a soap opera. My agents had asked me if I'd be interested in doing a recurring role of a psychiatrist on *The Young and the Restless*, which has been the highest-rated show for years. I thought, why not, I'll give it a shot, let me read the material. The material, as it turns out, was really good. And frankly there was more there, meat-wise, than in anything else I'd done. I thought this would be a fun acting exercise. I'll do it for the few weeks they wanted me for. In the beginning I found little tricks I could do to get myself noticed even more. Subtle looks at the leading lady, things like that. The producers and directors thought that was interesting, different, so they made the character a regular. I had such a great story line. Even the very first year I was on it, I got nominated for an Emmy. That sort of said something to me that you don't have to be all about looks on a soap opera. Everyone I was working with, however, were these beautiful people. Some of them were good actors, some of them were not. It worked. Soap operas are acting. You get to work on a full character that goes on day after day after day. You've got to work on your toes almost like repertory theater. So it's very rewarding.

Willie C. Carpenter: Soaps are the hardest job to do in TV; it's work. You're constantly learning lines, particularly if you have a part. If you have a recurring role and they are writing for you in every episode this week, you're essentially saying the same thing every day but with two or three words that are different. It's work. I liked it, but it is one job in the industry that if I had another option, I'd take it. It's all-consuming, it takes everything you've got. When I was in there for every episode you have to go home and learn lines. First thing in the morning you go to the set, they want you ready. You get no help on the set. No help from directors. You walk through—you have a little chat, a little blocking, and if you don't know what the hell you are doing, you're in trouble. I really found that was the toughest because you didn't have any help. Once they do the blocking they go up into the [control] booth [Directors leave the stage and go into a room where there are monitors for all the cameras. They communicate with the actors over a loudspeaker.], and now you are listening to the voice of God. You are really swimming on your own then.

Rif Hutton: Expect to do take after take after take after take, to the point [*laughs*] I can't believe it. When you're doing a commercial, you're not the star—the star is whatever that product is. They will shoot that sucker over and over again until they get that product to look exactly right. On a film set or a TV show, you basically have the director or producer running the thing. On a commercial you've got the client, the company that's producing it, and they give notes in between every take. So it is very common to do the simplest of things. Pick up a chicken wing and bite into it twenty times. That's the nature of commercials. It's [getting cast] so random, you have to grin and go with it. You are just there to service a product—you can't let your ego get in the way, certainly not with commercials.

Nestor Carbonell: I remember auditioning for a ketchup commercial; I thought, wow, I might have a shot at this one. They are looking for this guy and my agent is pumping me up, and sure enough I show up and there are one hundred guys who look not too different than I do. [*laughs*] There is a lot of competition out there. That is the first shocker—there are a lot of people wanting to do the same thing you want to do. I quickly learned that with commercial work, there is a gift and a talent for it: like sitcom, there is a different sensibility than in dramatic work. It is slightly more heightened—not so much that it's extremely broad, but there is a level of energy there. It can be its own art, its own technique. There was an element of chance there, looks and all these other variables, it is much more prevalent in commercials. It can be a numbers game. I said, I can't take this too personally; it's the first thing I learned. They send you out a lot and expect to get a lot of rejections because there are thousands vying for that job.

Willie C. Carpenter: I think for commercials it's knowing who you are, willing to be silly, not worrying about how you look. If you have some kind of personality, that's a warm personality—it doesn't have to be that, but for me they were all silly, they were all fun. They are not serious and bigger than life. I had that friendly personality that I knew that people liked. It was just the way it worked. The commercial business is now using real people. I think it is a matter of constantly attacking the industry, the casting people. I did groom myself to be that all-American kind of guy. The biggest thing at the time, I think I looked like a lot of people physically, visually like people that were working—Jim Brown, Bill Cosby. People saw that hint of somebody they recognized and I think that worked in my favor. I knew that, so I promoted that.

Magda Harout: I think you have to be more flexible acting in commercials because you don't have time to really develop a character. You are given the words, you have this situation, and you do it. You don't take that seriously. I think you have to have a sense of humor doing commercials because what's important is the residuals you get. Remember the idea is not you, you're serving the role of selling a product. That's your job and you do it. You can get a great deal of satisfaction from it. And they have great catering! [*laughs*]

Marianne Muellerleile: So then you've got the series job and that is wonderful for many reasons, but paramount, you really are part of the family. You are privy to so much more information as to how a show works. You begin to know all the writers, six, eight of them. All the producers who all have input into the production and sometimes into the very role you're playing. You also begin to understand how the network tries to influence the production. Of course the production company molds the product. You have the studio. You have these three entities with lots and lots of people in each group. You begin to see so much more of the business. You also begin to wonder how it gets done. There are so many voices who are contributing to the process and many of them should not be. Because they are not talented and they are not artistic. . . . they are so business-oriented. That's kind of crushing. There's an aspect of being in a series setting that is a little crushing. The people doing the show really want to make a great show. Produce something the public will enjoy, enrich their lives. But there are so many entities working against it. It's been really enlightening.

Clyde Kusatsu: Life is much better when you are a series regular. It's a little bit more hectic. Lot of times you may be doing the last day of shooting and you haven't had time to read the next day's episode to learn what it is about. There is more pressure to come into [things] as a guest. To hit the ground running and to fit in. Your job is to make it run well. In an hour situation the Pooh-Bahs are the regulars. They're the ones who are catered to. You're there to help the story along and make them look good. That's what your job is, not to shine as a bright star to be discovered. What I like about one-hour is that it's also a challenge to be more real, more natural, and not be artificial. Half-hour you tend to be more a little theatrical, a little bit broader. You have to have a combination of both. The funny parts when you have to be funny—you have to be broad enough, physical-timing-wise to do the joke, to set it up, to deliver the punch line or the reaction situation. When it becomes a tender moment, a real moment, when the audience goes "awww," then you really have to go to an honest point of being natural too. It's more sunshiny in a half-hour.

Amy Hill: A successful voice-over artist is basically a good actor. The training that I had in improvisation—you don't have time to work on the scripts; you show up and the scripts are sitting there. It's learning to listen and react honestly. Realizing all of the emotion is going to be in your voice. You cannot depend upon your face, you cannot depend upon your mannerisms, you can't depend on anything but your voice. You learn to focus your energy on that. The better you are as an actor, the better you are in voice work. I didn't do a lot of character stuff that I did in improv because nobody ever asked me to. Many producers said I didn't have a funny voice. I believed in myself and now I do cartoon work primarily as an Asian voice. I depend on characters that I have done in the past and I do depend upon my improvisational work.

Ashley Gardner: You can be so creative [with voice work]. You get to play all these different kinds of characters you'd never be able to play. Nobody cares what you look like; you can show up in your pj's and do it, nobody is going to care. If you are lucky enough to get on a great, great show, like *King of the Hill*, where the writing is superb and all the people there are really nice, that makes it especially good. When you are an actor, you depend a lot on your face to get out the emotion you are trying to give. You do have to consider that you can't rely on the physical. It is all in your voice. You get a feel for it after you do it for a while.

CHAPTER SIX

Making the Transition from Stage to Film

Good acting, either on stage or in film, is a willingness to behave with a strong personal sense of truth. It requires an ability to tap into your imagination, your inner life, to make a connection with your instrument, to have a command of language and an intuitiveness of being in the moment. Actors then make specific choices based on the material in regard to given circumstances, place, character relationships, and objectives in the scene. Then, by living off the other actors, you create rehearsed and spontaneous moments that bring the scene to life. The more you are able to use your vulnerabilities and strength, humor, honesty, physical appearance, and imagination, the more appealing an actor you become. Depending upon the material and the format, actors then use that part of themselves that is needed to fulfill the requirements of the scene. This holds true in whatever medium you are working in. The *technical* aspects of working in film, episodic television, sitcoms, or commercials can easily be understood. It is therefore important to have a solid foundation of acting technique.

The greatest difference between acting on film and on the stage is the intimacy of film. Without having to vocally and physically project to the last row in the theater eight shows a week, actors in film develop an ability to stay within themselves and allow the camera to capture their behavior and emotional state of being. That means an actor is working from that very honest place from within, and can do less (project out), while the camera just a few feet away from him lays hold of his performance. In a scene where you have a close-up or share a two-shot, your face fills the entire frame. Therefore the smallest of gestures and behaviors are magnified tenfold. It is not a matter of being small, but an ability to trust your instrument and know that what you have chosen to do will be there. Playwrights write monologues that stage actors love to perform that describe what a character is thinking. In film an audience can look into your eyes and see your character's private thoughts and emotional state of being register throughout your body. Film work allows you to *be*, to breathe, to think, to respond; it gives an added dimension to your story-telling possibilities.

Another contrast between acting for the stage and in film is rehearsal time. A veteran stage actor loves to rehearse over an extended period of time to develop her character and relationships within the play. And even when a play opens, the work continues to grow. At the end of the day there are notes from the director that an actor can mull over before the next rehearsal. A stage actor has control over his performance from the moment the curtain goes up until the final bow. In film you will find it is your responsibility to come to work prepared from day one. That means all strong choices for your character must already be made. Any dialect work, any physicality, the emotional life, the relationships with the other characters all have to be accessible from the moment filming begins. There is no time for you to discover it weeks into filming. However, within each scene, each take, you will be able to look to discover something new about the event as if you are performing it for the first time, every time. By giving the editor many choices in a scene, you allow her to sculpt your performance in postproduction with the director to tell the story in the best possible way. Many new actors have the misconception that when they act with a professional film director, he will share his brilliant directing ideas with them about how to act. Most likely, when working actors report to a set on the first day of shooting, they will have never met the other cast members and will have established no previous relationships. The director will hopefully know what he wants to shoot, and how to set up the shot and blocking, and then you are for the most part on your own. A few film directors who come with a theater background and a budget that allows for it may have you in for a table read and limited rehearsal before actual filming begins. I volunteer for the Screen Actors Guild Foundation Conversation Series in Los Angeles, where I have the opportunity to interview the higher-profile actors in our union. On different occasions I interviewed Hilary Swank and Kevin Bacon, both who were recently directed by the legendary actor and director

Clint Eastwood. They both described how Clint expected his actors to be prepared, ready to shoot, having made whatever character choices that were necessary before filming began. Kevin spoke of the research he did on his own with the local police department and about hiring a voice coach for his Boston dialect in *Mystic River*. Hilary trained for three months as a boxer and brought in different jump-rope routines that were used in *Million Dollar Baby*. There was no rehearsal time other than what the actors worked on independently beforehand. As for episodic television, a guest star will get little or no direction. Usually you'll hear, "Let's do it again, this time faster, with more energy, but do less." I kid you not! An actor with technique will know how to take result-oriented direction and turn it into something constructive for himself.

When working on the stage, by the time you are into performance, your costume, makeup, and blocking are finalized. You have your part memorized backward and forward, and when you are off stage, you're ready to make your entrance, concentrated and in the moment. Compare this with shooting on film. Right before you are about to start filming, there will be a wardrobe person adjusting your clothing, a makeup person powdering your face, a script supervisor going over your dialogue, a cameraperson asking you not to block the other actors' light—all at the same time! In addition, when you are placed in front of the camera, there may be fifty or more people standing behind the camera, waiting to shoot the scene. To remain relaxed before someone calls "action," I suggest you take a moment for yourself, breathe, and calmly take in all the activity around you. Simultaneously you're juggling your inner concentration on the scene at hand. Stay focused on what you are there to do. Check to make sure you are breathing. Commit to your choices and go for it. If a spontaneous moment occurs, let it lead you and be willing to improvise if need be. The joy of acting on film is living fully through a moment and being able to repeat it while making additional discoveries as you work.

Another difference a stage actor needs to adapt to while working on film is the lack of audience feedback while you are performing. On stage you develop a sense of how the performance is going and you can live off that energy. In film there is you, the other actors, the director, and the crew on the set. It is counterproductive to try to grab the attention of anyone behind the camera in evaluating your performance. Through experience you will be able to honestly judge how well you are working.

As a veteran actor I rarely ask questions of the director. I go about my work with my intentions and if something is missing, I trust that the director will approach me and tell me what is missing, and then I will make the necessary adjustments. If no one says anything to you, just keep doing what you were doing because you must be doing something right. There is no applause at the end of filming a scene (The accolades come later on when what you have filmed is aired on television or in the movie theaters and you hear from your family and friends); the reward is in doing the work. A wise actor will have self-appreciation and satisfaction because she came in prepared, worked as well as she could, and made some discoveries in the process, even if the only thing she hears from the director is "Good, got it! Let's move on."

Jack Kehler: You have to completely take responsibility for your own arena, for what you have been hired for. Be prepared, know your lines. Be ready to go with whatever is going to be. Unlike stage, you don't really rehearse in the way you are probably used to. So you really have to know what you are doing, what your character is doing. What the gist of the scene is. It's so much preparation. With stage, you prepare and go on. I don't find it that much different with film and TV. To me you are walking on stage, it's a performance. The difference is that it's much smaller. The camera is two, three feet away from you, so you don't have to be so big. You really have to trust whatever you're thinking, whatever you're doing in the smallest way is fine. I always keep saying to myself, "Dare to be boring." You just have to trust that the little things that you are doing, the camera is picking it up. And relaxation. You hear it a million times, the more relaxed you can be, the more in your space with the people around you. Don't put walls up so you can be in your thing. Include everything. I just try to take in everything that is going on around me, without losing what is going on with me and my character. And breathe. It's so simple, but boy it's really what it comes down to.

Roxanne Hart: Acting for the camera has been about learning how to relax and allowing that thought process to occur while the camera is running. To actually have "the thought," to actually have that thought move across your face. For me it has been about less interference, less control.

It's also been about learning what your stage is. Instinctually from the get-go, I had good stage legs, in that I understood what the picture was. I understood that if I'm standing in front of an audience and my foot was tapping that the audience saw that picture. Whatever emotional situation that I was in I could reveal my state of being through my whole body. You have to understand where the camera is and what the camera is seeing, and that takes a while. Unless you instinctually do understand the medium. I was a much, much better stage actor than I was a film actor. I think I'm better at it now. I would say for me it's about relaxing, it's about understanding the material as much as I can. It's about undressing emotionally in a way. It's about allowing the camera in.

Maria Canals: The camera sees everything that you are thinking. Not [just] everything you are saying and doing. You have to be totally present in your eyes. Just being, rather than portraying and doing—just being. Sometimes that is hard to do when you are used to theater. I would say to be totally, totally present in the character and in the moment. To have fun. There is no such thing as big and small. When you are emotionally there—for real—it's not big. Look at Al Pacino. Stay away from bigger, smaller. Smaller for film, bigger for the theater. Not necessarily. Be emotionally there.

Barry Primus: When you look at superb [trained] acting, Kim Stanley, Marlon Brando, James Dean, all the people like that, you see there is a certain state of being. While the action is important, and while intentions are important, good actors always work on two levels, great actors work on four levels, six levels. I decided in the movies that I would stay with these inner things that I built for myself, and to relate from them. I had a lot of private thoughts on film. I would just sit there with my private thoughts and I went where they went. I think Marlon Brando said, "Acting is easy. You just have to listen to the partner and his intention, what his intention is. Analyze it correctly. Forget the mythology and respond."

April Grace: The biggest transition is understanding the audience is two inches from your face. You don't tell them the story the same way that you tell an audience which is rows and rows away. Most of the things for me were technical—trying to fill the space with my voice when there are microphones everywhere. I did four student films and what I would recommend for someone to get the feel of what it [acting on film] is like is to find student filmmakers. That way you get to see yourself on film in situations that won't be detrimental to your career. There is so much subtlety to storytelling that you can do with film that you can't do on stage. If you can see yourself enough and watch yourself, then you can figure out for yourself what you are doing and what you need to do differently.

Luck Hari: For me it's much more of a challenge than theater. With theater there is always a bag of tricks that [work] for me; I don't have that bag of tricks when I'm in front of a camera. I have to be much smaller. I don't have to worry about hitting the back row of a twelve-hundred-seat house. I feel the camera doesn't lie. That is much more difficult. When I am working on television and film I have to totally 100 percent remind myself to breathe and to connect with the other actor. If I can accomplish those two things, I'm well on the road.

Robin Bartlett: Being as much yourself—along with all the accoutrements that you put on to make a character. Once that has been taken care of, to have it happen as much as though for the first time. How you trick yourself in doing that is the way to do it. On film what gets picked up are all kinds of reactions and small expressions that you don't even know you are doing. If you try to plan them all out, you would look terribly false. It really is a matter of leaving yourself alone. Being as unselfconscious as possible.

Brent Jennings: I really like acting for the camera, particularly film acting, because it is not shot in continuity; most times it's like putting a puzzle together. You know that this piece has got to fit with this piece. I enjoy that. I remember coming up with this adage in my mind that the difference between film and stage was that thought is active. The idea that in film your thoughts can be as active and as loud as shouting in a proscenium stage. Because the camera has the capacity to see what you're feeling, what you're thinking. So it's really important for you to really be inside a character. In a way you can't get away with some things on film that you can get away with on stage. On stage, your stage technique can sometimes cover the fact that you are not really feeling a certain kind of thing in the moment. Nobody's looking in your eyes. Nobody is really seeing your soul. On film you can't lie. The director can cheat for you. If you have to break down and cry and you can't do it, he can come back a little bit or shoot off another angle. They can cover for you. Film has the capacity to be so immediate. If you can think it, if you can start with how this character thinks from moment to moment, and really get into the inner life of that character, most times you are going to have a performance that is really going to be right on the money. You really don't have to speak on film to be effective.

Shelley Morrison: It's capturing the character's behavior. Not all your acting abilities come out when you're talking; most of it is coming out when you are listening. It's being there, moment to moment. Film is a slower process. It's learning how to marshal your energy level. It's the behavior because the camera will pick up just the slightest thing.

Miguel Sandoval: That formal sort of physical training [pantomime] that I had provides one with a terrific kinesthetic awareness and a great kinesthetic memory. It is extremely important if you are working in film and television. When you go from the wider shot to the close-up, the script person and the director—especially if they have gotten something good from the master—want to see it replicated as you move in closer and closer to the face. That mime training that provided me with that kinesthetic memory helps me to duplicate what I have done in previous takes, while keeping it alive and fresh, keeping it real. It is not something I have to think about. That sort of dancer's training, if you will, puts into your musculature, puts it into your body. Then you automatically do it again while intellectually you can explore the content of the words you are saying and the actions you are doing.

Amy Hill: In sitcoms there are four cameras usually. It is their job to catch me. They give me marks—I can hit my marks—I am not conscious of the camera. There are so many cameras. Sometimes a director in the course of rehearsal—you have four days to rehearse—the director will say, this will be the only camera that will be on you for this scene, so be aware of that. Otherwise if they don't say anything, I am working with the other actors. In film there is that one camera and it is relentlessly on you. There is nothing like having that single where you can feel every bead of sweat and your big giant face is going to be on that screen. In the film world you really feel that you have to be so honest; in other mediums you can pretend and try to get away with it, but in film I have to be really honest.

Lucinda Jenney: The thing that is so important [about] having a theater background is that you have years of getting the feel of having to do it for yourself. You don't get that chance if you haven't gone through a rehearsal process. [Acting on film], you take your homework, the same techniques, same thinking, but you do it by yourself. You arrive [on the set] being your own director and then you give it up to the director you meet. I'm my own director when it comes to movies and television. But I'm my own director with the knowledge that I might get fired because they don't like what I have chosen to do.

James Rebhorn: One of the advantages to contemporary film for the actor is that they are filmed on location and the environment is a tremendous source of inspiration for the actor. Because it is on location, it is given to you. On a set, even if it's on a sound stage, you have to work harder to create that. It's all fabrication, it's all pretend. I find generally, the directors that I most like to work with are the directors that have some experience in the theater. They generally have experience of working with dramatic material that has to do with human behavior as opposed to cinematic effect. Not all directors are like that. The other directors I like working with are the ones that have been editors. They have seen everything and somehow they have a sensibility of dealing with actors.

Debra Monk: It was a real journey for me. It has taken me many, many years to really feel comfortable and kind of know what I am doing. I still feel like I'm not always savvy, like some of those actors who know every single thing about filmmaking. I did learn that the same way I work on a role in the theater is the same way I work on a role in the movies. It's no different for me. What the difference is [is] technical. For example, when I worked with Dennis Franz [*NYPD Blue*], he was the one who taught me that if you have a big speech you don't have to go in thinking you have to do the whole speech perfectly. They can do pickups. I didn't know that, I saw him do that. He didn't get the first part of the speech—he messed up—they said, we'll pick it up from there. I didn't understand that. For me it was a huge burden lifted—I try to do it all—but you know that if you mess it up they can just start from there. There are things like that they can edit, which are a huge gift for an actor. When you are doing a play, the audience is responsive, it's a comedy, you can feel it. I don't always know and I've always just trusted my director. That has given me a lot less stress.

Armin Shimerman: It is essential to work in front of the camera and monitor your results later on. The camera is really about looking into the windows of the soul of the actor, which is the eyes. Seeing what is in them. It is imperative that you work in front of the camera and learn. The greatest class you can take is to become a recurring character [you may apply this when you are involved in a low-budget film or TV project]. With a recurring character you can build on your performance—you can six or eight weeks later say, "What did I do right, what did I do wrong? What do I believe when I'm watching this?" You have to look at the episode two or three times so you get over what you look like. About the fourth time, you start to really look at what the acting is about. You think, "When I was doing that, it was too much. Why is so much of me in three-quarters; why wasn't I looking more towards the camera?" These are things you learn so the next time you take some of the lessons you learned watching that first episode and you apply them. Gradually you remember what you did and you adjust, you sculpt, you reposition, you learn. You become a better actor by doing that.

Anne-Marie Johnson: One of the tools I learned through osmosis—I was never taught this at school—was being silent with your face, your expression. Not being silent audibly but having a quiet body. It comes in handy for close-ups and two-shots. They really want you to work with your eyes, your mouth. Just the slightest movement with your head says something else. It's really calming and quieting in the body. Actors are very demonstrative and animated, and that doesn't work in single-camera work. I had to bottle that natural energy of mine and contain it and let it work out in my speech. It was a very difficult trick to learn how to control that physical energy and place it someplace else. It took years to train myself not to be so animated.

Anne DeSalvo: Realize the camera is your friend. Make it real, make your feelings real. Don't go outside of it—stay inside the work. Sometimes they have courses [on] acting for the camera, I don't know how much I believe in that—my feeling is good work is good work and you make the adjustment. When you go to the set, you have to be very prepared. You have to have made choices. It's not going to be sitting around and "Let me try this, let me try that." Especially in television, you memorize the lines, you go there, and you do it. Very often the director doesn't even say anything to you. Obviously he must be liking what you are doing, but in my experience they don't say too much. Make choices! There is nothing more boring and dull and ineffective than an actor who acts in generalizations. The more specific it is, the more interesting because the more personal it becomes.

Richard Fancy: The thing that really struck me when I started working in film was how technical it is. Film looks like life and theater is so . . . theatrical. There are a lot of technical demands. You mustn't overlap in a close-up. [The actor whose close-up is being shot must have his dialogue recorded cleanly, without the off-camera actor speaking over his lines.] You have to match, but actually you don't have to match everything. You should have some notion of what it is you have to match. You have to match when you are sitting down, or picking up a glass, for example. A friend of mine . . . , a director, used to say when an actor did a very interesting piece of work with a lot of movement that evolved during the scene . . . , "That's brilliant and you're going to hate yourself in twenty-five minutes." The whole spontaneity thing particularly if you're not a star—if you're a star and you don't match, they will cut away to the character actor who is matching. [Matching on film means to repeat behavior that has been established from a previous take. For example, taking off your eyeglasses on a specific line. That action will need to be repeated every time the scene is filmed.]

Ashley Gardner: I do find that theater actors [are] more interesting to watch on film. They have been used to more dense material, dealing with the subtext of the character, the back story, which you don't get in TV crap and a lot of bad movies. You are able to imbue what you don't get from a script from your imagination from the years of doing it through theater. You can bring that with you into acting on camera. That's a great thing, a really great thing.

Erick Avari: I was able to make the adjustments as I went along. There are a lot of differences, the stop-and-go. The fact you have to keep your concentration; on stage it's so much easier, it flows, even if you're not on stage you're stepping back into that. While the camera is rolling, while they were slating [the moment before filming begins, a camera assistant stands with a clapboard to identify the scene and take for the editor], I'd try to go back in time and get a running start into the scene.

Juanita Jennings: I never worry where the camera is. To this day I still don't. It's about the truth of the moment for me. I think if you're in the moment, that's what the DP [director of photography] will pick up. They do their job, you do yours.

CHAPTER SEVEN

You're Working; You're Not Working

To survive in this business, actors have to develop skills to cope with the insecurity of unemployment, fear, the constant rejection, and the pitfalls of success if they are to have longevity with their careers. That is no small task. Unless you are able to overcome these obstacles, you will be driven away from your passion. Time and time again you will be tested. How much do I want to do this? What psychological price am I willing to pay so that I can remain in the game? Those that keep focused on their goals and are willing to live through the heartbreak and make the necessary sacrifices are the ones who will remain at the end of the day.

Something you will have to adapt to right from the start is the euphemism of being "in-between jobs." It is a positive spin on a very serious problem. If you are in need of money, then first and foremost you have to get a survival job. Never feel you have to make any excuses for working; there's nothing dishonorable in it. Being broke and unable to pay the rent is no way to live. You do not need to suffer. You need to support yourself. Always remember that your commitment is to being an actor and that the survival work should be temporary and flexible so you can keep on auditioning. Don't lose sight of your intended goal, which is to act. Even actors who are able to pay their bills solely by acting may actually be performing only a few days or weeks out of the year. There is constant downtime in the life of an actor. It is important to use this time and remain inventive. Actors should be taking classes to widen their perspective on life and to hone their craft. Learn to paint, write, teach, direct, play an instrument, anything that will keep your creative juices flowing. If the opportunity arises, start a business. Volunteer for a cause that you believe in. By focusing on something outside yourself and your career, you can use your downtime constructively. Negative, destructive behavior does nothing to advance your career or your craft. Suffering will not make your a better actor. It is tough enough to be an actor and the last thing you want to do is wallow in self-pity.

Landing acting work goes in cycles no matter how successful you become. Hopefully there will be times when nearly every audition results in your getting the job, and you can go from one booking to the next. When this good fortune occurs, ride it out without thinking about it for as long as possible. For just when you believe you have got it made, the door may close. You go back to wondering if you will ever get cast again. You're auditioning as well as before but nothing is coming your way. This is the time to have faith in your ability and know that what goes around comes around. If you choose how to spend this time wisely, you can make the unemployed periods productive.

Fear destroys an artist. The fear of failure and success. The fear of criticism. The fear of being seen. They are all psychological concerns that prevent an actor from being whole and fulfilling her potential. It stifles your instrument during an audition, prevents you from giving it your best shot. You break out into the sweats when performing, making a once natural task an unpleasant experience. Uncomfortable feelings sneak up on you when working on challenging material so that you want to shut down. When you begin to acknowledge your fears, you are then able to harness them and make them a useful addition to who you are. As you welcome that part of yourself to the work, you open the door to the endless creative possibilities that exist for an actor.

What makes actors so special, and the reason the public will pay to see us on stage and in film, is our ability to express the human condition with all its complexities in a creative way. It is a gift that we possess, but we must allow ourselves to reveal it. An actor has to choose to want to be truly seen. To be open and available. To stand emotionally naked before a group of strangers and to know that it's safe to do that. A trustworthy and experienced acting teacher coupled with a willingness on your part will help you break through those barriers and develop the craft to be able to be open. By learning how to breathe through a moment, you afford yourself the opportunity to get to the other side—as difficult or as painful as it might be. When you shut down and hold on to that fear, you are denying your own personal sense of truth. When confronted with this challenge, actors can choose to flee by making all kinds of excuses, or they can see it as an opportunity for growth. The more you make friends with it, the easier dealing with your fear becomes. I have to admit I hardly know an interesting, complicated actor who hasn't gone through some kind of personal therapy to tackle these issues, myself included. The more you are willing to invest in yourself, the more you have to offer—and the healthier you become as a person.

All actors must face up to the fact that no matter how prepared they are or how well they audition, they may not get a role they so desperately want. It is understandable to feel rejected and dispirited. With so much of the process out of your hands, it is hard to see that the law of supply and demand holds true. For that one role you believe you are so right for, the casting director, producer, director, agency, studio, or network will have an unlimited supply of actors to choose from. You sign in for a commercial audition and there are from twenty-five names to countless pages of actors auditioning for that one role. While you are waiting at a theatrical audition, you recognize the faces of several more-established actors vying for the same part as you are. You psych yourself out before you have even gone into the room to audition.

Not getting work or, even worse, not auditioning at all wears on the soul and tears at your own sense of self-worth. You feel as if you are carrying the weight of the world on your shoulders. A sense of blame or doubt colors your world because you're not able to accomplish what you so dearly want to do. It is very hard, no matter how you try, not to take the rejection personally. But that is exactly what you must avoid to survive! You must accept that it is not personal, it's only business. Recognize that it's a numbers game. The more times you get out there, the better the chance you have of your number coming up. If you weigh yourself down by asking, "What is wrong with me?" and let your spirit be broken, you are dismissing everything else about who you are. Your loving relationships, your outside interests, what your friends and associates admire about you do not change. Hopefully they are there to be supportive, to encourage you to dust yourself off and get back in there. The best thing that you can do is recognize the loss and find something constructive to do with yourself that enables you to get past it. Whatever cliché, poem, song, or piece of literature helps you express your disappointment, use it. I'll recite a Shakespearean soliloquy out loud to vent my feelings. Go out for a walk, visit a museum, exercise, do anything constructive, but go through it and let it go. Then cinch up your belt and get back on that horse. There is no denying that this is a difficult task. But that is the psychological price that you have to pay for having chosen to be an actor and wanting to be a survivor in this business.

Hopefully there will come a time in your career when you can earn your living doing what you love to do: acting. When you reach this moment through hard work, dedication, and talent, you should consider yourself a successful working actor. For some this will occur from a single job that keeps them employed for an extended period of time and pays them enough money to live on. For others it will be an accumulation of work and residuals (love those checks in the mailbox!) that means they no longer need an outside job. Whatever situation you find yourself in, relish this good time. Appreciate how far you have come and how much you have invested of yourself to be called a working actor. To be able to reach this level of success, remembering the days when you first set out on this path, is an achievement to be quite proud of. Savor this opportunity, for it won't last forever! Unless you earn a star's salary that financially sets you up for life, or you are lucky enough to win the lottery, *you had better save your money.* Create a rainy-day fund to draw upon when the work cycle has you wondering when you will ever work again. That is the reality of show business.

Money will give you security and freedom to have more artistic choices. It will hold you over during lulls in the business. Money will take away the worries of how you will pay the rent. What success, money, and fame won't do is make you a happier person. If you get caught up with the superficial aspects of the business, you may lose focus on your passion, which should be your work. Continue to be gracious and grateful for your good fortune. Use your money to invest in yourself by continuing to grow as an artist. Actors love to complain when they are not auditioning, not working, and even when they are working. Having a successful acting job comes with its own problems and responsibilities. When you're on a television series, you want to know why they aren't writing more for your character. When you're working on location, you have to circumvent a star's ego while being away from home for a long period of time. A commercial actor gets overly exposed and casting agents don't want to call him in for an audition. If you remain grounded in who you are, you'll be able to withstand the temptations that come with being a success.

❖ ❖ ❖ ❖

Mary Pat Gleason: Actors have a hard job ahead of them. The muscles to take on rejection at the rate you should be taking it on, because you should be going out after things and struggling to get things. Which means if you are really doing that on a day-to-day basis, you're getting rejection on a day-to-day basis as much as success. You have to get a really tough inner core that believes that this is your calling. I needed to know it was my calling. It couldn't be just a career, it's too tough as a career; I could go back to nursing anytime. When I realized this is a calling and I might have something to say of some import, that helped me whenever I was up against difficulty. Or even a year of unemployment, which can happen after many years of lots of employment and good money, wonderful jobs and lots of support. You may all of a sudden find yourself with a year where you cannot find work. If you believe in your heart that's where you're supposed to be, you can do any kind of survival job. You can hang in there. It will come around again. There's a rhythm to this business. Most of us don't know that either. That's hard to tell a young person because they don't want to hear it. But there is a rhythm. You work a lot and then you don't work. If you want to see that, you can take a look at any celebrity. You'll see years where we saw tons of film from them or a lot of television and they disappear for a while. And they have to sustain themselves and some of them can't and they drift out of the business.

Stephen Mendillo: There's so much of it. Nothing but fear, uncertainty, insecurity, rejection—those are the four. That's all the acting business is, in one sense. Of course, it's a lot of other things, but it's rife with that. I believe it's the antithesis to what's necessary. That actors need to be supported, need positive reinforcement. They need encouragement. These are the things that actors need. They don't need so much of what they in fact do get. A lot of times directors are so mean to actors and actresses, tearing them down. It is the last thing the creative gestation process needs. It needs the exact opposite. I abhor it. I think it's terrible. There is plenty of it, there's too much of it. I'm finding actually it a little less and less as time goes on, that there is a little bit less than in the, quote, "older school." These days there seems to be a little more touchy-feely, user-friendly stuff. They need enrichment, encouragement and they can do amazing things. Why not, then? Of course so much of the world that we live in, so much of the theater and television is mediocre. We should always be getting above mediocrity. You can't ask people to come down to the theater that is mediocre. To go through all the trouble and to pay for it and it's mediocre. This needs encouragement, this needs positive reinforcement. I abhor this kind of rejection and discouragement and so forth.

Sheila Kelley: Rejection is a good thing and it's a bad thing. Because if you put all your eggs in this basket, which you have to do to succeed, you are going to get devastated and hurt a lot. Which I was. And when you take all of your eggs out of that basket, that seems when you work a lot more. That's when people come pounding your door down because you are not pounding their door down anymore. All of a sudden you have a little cock to your walk. You are not playing their game of "reject me, take me, take me, don't take me, accept me." That to me just breeds mediocre work. Fear can be paralyzing. I think it is a horrible thing for acting. Whenever I walk into a room that instills fear in people, I often have wanted to get up and walk out. Finally last year I got up and I walked out. I said, "You know what, I'm not right for this role. I am going to go now." It was the most empowering thing I have ever done. Otherwise you are powerless and become the victim as an actor. If you are a victim you are lost. You don't need to be a victim as an actor. You can be a motherfucker as an actor and they'll respect you more. Then they'll want you, when you say, I don't want you.

Ethan Phillips: I'm way beyond what I define [as] success. I love to act. And if I can pay my bills as an actor and have a little left over to go to a movie or take a vacation with my wife, that is success to me. Success was not being on the cover of *People* magazine, success was not being famous in really any way other than making a decent living doing what I loved. Working in good plays, hopefully in good films, TV—that's all I ever wanted. I just wanted to make a living. It was surprising to me to make some money, more money than I thought I would have made. I'm by no means rich; I have taken care of some financial insecurities that I had when I started out. Those are obstacles you can't think about. When I started out I never thought about making money. I never thought about being famous. I never thought about anything other than doing quality work that would earn the respect of my colleagues. I would be acknowledged as a player, somebody who knew what they were doing in this field, who was a true actor. A good actor.

Barry Shabaka Henley: If you know yourself you can walk into these situations where 99 percent of the time you are going to be rejected and not take it personally. If you are the kind of sensitive soul who takes it personally, this is not the business for you. You are going to get more rejection than acceptance. A casting director once said to me, "It's not about rejection, it's about selection. They selected somebody else, they didn't reject you." It's a process of selection. There's five different actors coming into a room and there are ten people making a decision. It's not personal. That is one thing a young actor is going to have to learn early: 90 percent of why you don't get a job will be out of your control. All you can do is your work. Come in prepared, come in with energy, come in with a positive attitude. I think that those who stay in acting are either masochistic fools or people who are on a spiritual journey. To be able to take rejection without humiliation—that's a spiritual evolution.

Shelley Morrison: I have a wonderful family. I have another life. I've had a myriad of other jobs. I've worked as a nurse, I've worked as a salesgirl, I've worked as a music engineer. I write. I have a family, I have an anchor. We have a very wonderful spiritual community. We follow the Lakota Sioux traditions. If anyone needs anything, we circle the wagons. Even when I didn't have the visibility that I have now, I was always involved in charity work. Volunteerism. This is the work. Acting is the work. Be prepared when you go for an audition for a job, that's the work. Knowing how to give an interview. How you treat the people you work with, the people you meet. So you have a life and you don't become bitter.

Richard Fancy: In my thirties I couldn't get arrested as an actor. It became clearer and clearer to me that I was so angry all the time and frightened. Which had something to do with being so angry all the time. I said I actually need to look into this. I went into psychoanalysis, which is not the option for every actor. The thing that I thought was most important when I saw him for the first time, I said, "I want to make a contract with you. I think I'm getting in my own way as an actor. I want to make a contract that's what this job is about. I want to be looking at that. I want you to give me an idea about how long it would take to see some progress in that area?" He said, "In three months you should begin to see something." And by God, I began to notice that in auditions. I was less filled with both fear and rage. I was better able to deal with the person who was directing me as someone who had an interest in the situation. That this wasn't mine or his, this wasn't a competition, this was a negotiation. I had an interest in this and so did he.

Klea Scott: I moved to Los Angeles directly out of school. I went right into a series regular on a CBS television show [*Brooklyn South*]. My entire class went to New York City and I was the only one who moved here. That show got canceled at the end of a year. Part of me did think that once you started working professionally, you just kept going. I thought this job leads to the next job, work begets work, and that's going to be it. Finally I broke in and all it took was that one. I thought, "My God, this is going to happen all the time." Even *Seinfeld* ends. Everybody at some point wraps [has a final day of shooting] at some time, and that's it. You're looking for your next job. It suddenly dawned on me this was the life I chose. Then I went back doing theater for no money, for my husband in Los Angeles, where nobody sees theater. I just came off this TV show, this isn't how it's supposed to work, is it? I thought it was a stepping-stone towards security. There was this big lightbulb that said, you will never have job security because you have chosen to be an artist. You have got to make your peace with this. This is your decision.

Lupe Ontiveros: When you have a strong self-esteem, a focus, then you can withstand the rejection, the continuous rejection. You're too tall, too short, you're too fat, you're too skinny, you're this, you're that. You're nose is crooked, whatever. You have got to go in there with some really basic grounded structure for yourself. And that is the way you live your life. It is going to be the rest of your life. Not just to get into SAG, not just to get the role. Too many actors that are new are banking on their little T and As and their beautiful looks. They feel they can bypass what we had to go through. I love to say to a young person, "I want to see you at my age, see where you're at, darling!"

Emily Kuroda: My first job was a guest star and I thought I had it made. I thought this is what it is going to be like, it was just going to go up from here. Well, it doesn't. For a while I was going out for one-liners and thought, this is not right, this is not how it should be. For an Asian American actor, I go out for everything from big things to small things. It is just a matter of making a living doing something you absolutely love. Getting paid for playing—every day I knock on wood—I am grateful to be one of the people who can do this.

Vic Polizos: Fear has probably motivated me to some extent. Fear of being alone, fear of not being recognized, fear of being nobody, the fear of being poor. Those motivate me. The rejection has kept me from being a better actor. I have let it interfere with my work both in front of the camera and on stage. I've become too involved with what the people out there are going to think of me. It keeps me from allowing myself to fly— to be free as an actor, to be able to express myself. You have to let a lot of that stuff go and take the chances if you are really going to soar as an actor. As I got more successful, I found that became a bigger pressure.

Sheila Kelley: Success is being able to feed your face, being able to eat, being able not to have to do another job. A successful professional actor is someone who doesn't have to do any other job. A successful creative actor—that's ephemeral, that's so fleeting, so difficult. Some of the most untrained actors that I have ever met are some of the most gifted that I have ever met. Yet they'll never be on TV, never be in the movies. They don't have the soul for it. Some of the most gifted actors I know are too precious, too raw to survive what it takes to make it in Hollywood or on Broadway in the theater. It breaks my heart that the common person will never see them because they get broken here.

Christine Estabrook: I used to have a great fear of the word *action* when the camera starts to roll. I was always afraid if I forgot my lines, I would be pointed and laughed at. I've seen old actors do it over [request to reshoot a scene] and ask for another and another take in television. If they don't get it as a whole, they'll get it in pieces. It [fear] has taken me a long time, you know it is going to happen, you are going to get nervous— your mouth is going to get dry—so I put Vaseline on my teeth, that way my lips don't stick to my teeth. I know my lines as well as I can know them. You just walk [in] there and if your hand is shaking, put it on something, ground yourself. If you need a prop in your hand, get a heavy prop so it doesn't start shaking with your hand. I know I'm going to be nervous so I just live with it.

Magda Harout: We all have had rejection and we still get rejection. You either fall into that abyss of psychological mutilation, "Oh God, why not, why didn't they?" Or you can take a few minutes and feel that pain and then *get over it*. Just get over it. You can't be that self-absorbed. OK, you didn't get it, then you say, "What did I do wrong?" Sometimes it's not that you did something wrong; sometimes they weren't looking for that. Maybe you didn't look it, maybe they were looking for someone else, maybe they wanted to cast a friend. You just never know. You can't take it personally. You must never take rejection personally.

Robin Bartlett: I have [a] certain amount of a fear of fame. I don't want to live a life where I can't go to the supermarket. Especially living in L.A.—all you have to do is have to be on TV once and people will notice you. I am grateful for the fact that I'm a character actor and I have lots of different experiences and people don't identify me with a very particular thing. So people will come up and say, "Did we go to camp together?" That's fine. I think our whole celebrity culture is very corrupting and an awful thing. I don't want to participate in it. In a certain sense that made me less ambitious than a lot of people. If you really, really go for stardom, that's what you are going for. To me that's not real life.

Maria Canals: Sometimes you don't get the job, several times in a row. That disappointment can stay with you. We can't live in that. We have to be a little crazy, a little overly optimistic, a little bit of a dreamer. You have to have great belief in yourself. The tendency, I have talked to my actor friends, is to protect yourself. A human defense is to not pour your soul and guts out at the next audition. It wasn't well received last time. So there is a tendency to protect yourself, which is death to an actor. The whole advantage that you have is you are special and unique. You have to put that out there. You have to put your heart on a platter. Even if they don't accept it, your job is to put your heart out on a platter. We have to remember to not protect ourselves. Not getting the part is the nature of the beast. There are so many parts for so many actors. Staying confident and remember that I'm still that girl that got that last part, that's still me. You are not going to be loved by everyone. You've got something to give, somebody will love it eventually.

Lauren Tom: When I was first starting out, every time I reached a plateau what I thought [was] what success would be, it wasn't. It didn't turn out to be what I imagined. I wanted to be in a Broadway play; I did three of them, that was very exciting—don't get me wrong—it didn't make me whole. When I moved to Los Angeles I thought all I wanted to be was on a sitcom and then I would be whole. That didn't work either. What made me whole was to have a whole life. I don't think I've ever been happier than I am now. I'm not making the most money I've ever made and I'm not superfamous. I've got two incredible kids, I'm married. When I finally made that decision to choose my life over my next job, it was unbelievably liberating. Having kids really put my life into focus. It was the moment, "Oh, I get it. It's not all about me." [*laughs*] There's only so much happiness you can squeeze out of having all your attention on yourself. It took me a while to get that. I think in your twenties that's what you are meant to be doing.

Randle Mell: There is a lot of mythology that we buy into about successful actors, famous actors, working actors. As you know my wife is a very successful actress and she struggles, she doesn't struggle with the same things . . . necessarily that I do. She still has to compete for parts. Go through long periods of unemployment, not getting the parts that she wants. It is on a different level but it's the same experience. You want to be working. I find that when I'm working I need a lot less therapy. [*laughs*] It just makes a difference being a working actor. I'm working on this play; I'm making zero money. I feel more alive and engaged in my life. I'm sweeter to my kids because I come home fulfilled. Tired, fulfilled, creative, so I'm not obsessing about little things around the house. I got more important things to think about, damn it, I'm a working actor.

CHAPTER EIGHT

All You Want Is an Opportunity

At every turn in the road an actor will be confronted with yet another obstacle to success. It is how we treat those challenges and turn them into opportunities that will make for an extended career. A given in this business is that the industry looks to typecast actors. You are put into categories and only a select few actors are ever able to escape those limits. Actors such as Dustin Hoffman, Meryl Streep, Johnny Depp, and Nicole Kidman get to create a broad range of characters and are routinely praised for being able to play such diverse roles. The rest of us working actors are more restricted according to type, based on physical appearance, age, and experience. When there is such an overabundant pool of performers, casting for the most part will choose an actor that is dead-on "type." There is not much an actor can do to fight that. Once you are pigeonholed as a mom, dad, nurse, doctor, nun, or priest, you'll more than likely get to play that same part over and over again. To make it interesting or challenging, your job as an actor will be to make choices that will differentiate this character from the last time you played a similar type. Even the dialogue will sometimes have a familiar ring to it. Many times while filming, I've had a déjà vu experience, believing that I have spoken this text before.

To safeguard yourself against becoming brain-dead, you can escape back to the theater to keep the instrument alive. Nothing better than to sink your teeth into a meaty character from a compelling play. Going back to acting class gives you the venue to explore another part of who you are, by taking on a character for which you wouldn't necessarily be cast in the professional world. Many actors will gladly participate in play readings with or without an audience and for no money, to keep their acting chops alive. As the natural progression of age occurs, we go from playing rebellious sons and daughters to playing concerned parents or from societal misfits to established members of the community. Perhaps you have the talent and craft that enable you to bounce back and forth between comedy and drama, affording you a greater range of employment opportunities.

Another given obstacle in the business is ageism. There is no denying this is a young person's game. The older you get, the younger everyone else seems and the less acting possibilities there will be. A wise actor will look to expand job-related opportunities for herself in advance. Rarely will an actor be able to earn a living solely by acting. That's why actors often have a hyphen in their job description. Actor–acting coach, actor-director, actor-writer. When I first began earning money as an actor, I began to train myself to become an acting teacher. This way I would be able to build an additional stipend doing something in the field that I love. When working as a series regular, some actors on a television show follow a director and are able to make a successful transition behind the camera. Actors have a great ear for natural dialogue and character development, which can lead them to becoming playwrights and screenwriters. When you are "in between jobs," you need to plan ahead for the upcoming challenge of growing older in this young person's business. Then again, if you haven't made it by the time you're thirty, it may just mean you still have to grow more into who you are. The good fortune of being a character actor is that you have a greater possibility for longevity in a career than does a beautiful ingenue. Good looks may get you in the door, but great talent will keep you coming back time and time again.

Actors of color face an additional obstacle. There are fewer opportunities in terms of projects and roles for which you can audition. The industry has certainly made progress in reflecting the culture that we currently live in. No matter what ethnic background you are, there are characters that need to be cast according to race. People of color are gaining more power in the establishment, and it's filtering its way down from the top as producers, writers, and directors create a more culturally diverse world in film and television. Barriers have come down: a character of color may now have a relationship with character of a different race. Paying customers and television audiences have more opportunity to view film and television based entirely on their own life experiences. However, actors of color still have fewer options.

An additional problem is that what is written and produced can at times be stereotypical of an entire group of people. An actor of color then has a personal dilemma. How do I balance wanting to act with a script or character that is stereotypical or racist? I want to put food on the table but not have to behave in a demeaning way. It is a conundrum that I personally have never had to face, but one which I have discussed with actors of color. Their words and experiences will speak for themselves. What I can say is that an actor has to be able to face himself in the mirror. You never want to degrade yourself, no matter what the situation, over an acting gig. You need to empower yourself by maintaining a personal code of dignity. There will be some roles you will just have to turn down. You may be able to have input into others as you develop the character and thereby change the outlook of a writer or director.

With all actors, typecasting becomes an issue, and the black woman becomes tired of playing a single parent, the Asian actor, a nondescript villain, and the Latino, a gang member. You must consider the project, where you are in your career, and how much you need the money to decide whether or not this is the right project for you. All actors of color whom I have spoken with talk eloquently of their personal responsibility to their own racial background. They are aware that what they choose to act in and who their characters are reflect back on their community. Many have a historical perspective of the actors that came before them and the obstacles they had to deal with in order to succeed.

What every actor wants to do is to act. That is the plain and simple fact of the matter. The restrictions that the industry puts on us all because of race, age, gender, sexuality, or disability have to be fought tooth and nail if one is to earn a living by acting. All of us must take a stand and not be prevented from attempting to do what we love because someone else wants to put us in a category that may not fit. The actor who has the vision to see beyond the limits imposed upon her, coupled with the courage to adapt to change, becomes an actor who can have a long and varied career.

❖   ❖   ❖   ❖

Miguel Sandoval: It [race] clearly affects you career. I have all kinds of opinions about it. I'm like every actor probably. I don't want to be limited by my gender, my height, my ethnicity, et cetera, et cetera. I've never considered myself an actor of color. But the ugly reality is that the industry categorizes everybody and everything. Whether you're an actor or a sound person or a cinematographer, everybody has a category. It's limiting, but at the same time, oh gosh, I guess what I've thought about it is that as much as I don't want to be considered a *Latino* actor, I have made a niche for myself as exactly that. So here's the question: Is it better for me as a *Latino* actor to be in competition with three or four other guys my own age? Or is it better for me to be a WASP actor from Kennebunkport, Maine, and be up against three hundred, four hundred other guys for the same part? Everybody's limited. Everybody has that albatross around their neck to deal with in some shape or form. I think you just deal with it, whatever it is. Having said that, I hate it when my agent or manager says these words to me (I hopefully have trained them now not to say that): "They've decided not to go ethnic on this role." What the hell does that mean? They decided to not go ethnic on this role. That will get my small hairs up big time.

Grant Albrecht: There are fifty-three million people in this country with disabilities. They are certainly not depicted on television. The jobs I have gotten—I play serious people, doctors, lawyers for the most part. The auditions are very few and far between. Nontraditional casting is what they call it when you think outside the lines. Though it is happening increasingly, there is not much of it. Don't expect any special compensation for having a disability or being a minority. You're not going to get it. There aren't special auditions allowed for you. Amazingly on one of my first auditions, when they were looking for a very good-looking DA type, thirty-five to forty [years old], I thought, how many can there be? I'm certainly getting this. I showed up [and] there were thirty-five guys there in wheelchairs with SAG cards, all that fit that specific demographic. I thought, you've got to be kidding me. The odds are not going to get any easier. You have to really need to do this and want to do this in a big way.

Mary Pat Gleason: I think we have to keep re-creating ourselves. I think the most interesting thing in my journey was at about thirty-five, I went back to acting class. The acting teacher asked me why I was here. I said, "The truth is I'm here because I had so much attention and so much support when I was around twenty-one. I was doing everything, getting the leads and people were calling and I had to refuse things." I said, "I think

I'm attached to twenty-one. I'm still acting from that place that worked. I'm thirty-five years old. I've got all these years of experience on this planet, and I'm a much more interesting woman. I don't think I'm bringing the full woman to the stage. I think I'm still trying to get that girl work. I've got better things to offer now. I've got a better gift. Deeper and richer stories I should have the courage to tell. I just need an arena where I can get my courage up." He said, "I think that's a brilliant answer to go to class." I kept that as my goal to constantly go back.

Willie C. Carpenter: In the past, there haven't been a whole lot of parts for people of color in TV shows. If there is a black show, you figure you got a good shot at something. But there are eighty thousand other black folks who are thinking the same thing. It's the same as the rest of society. They're hiring, you get hired; they're not hiring, you won't get hired. I know who I am. I just try to get the job, whatever it is. I have to focus on what the industry is doing. Where I might be able to get a job. Where things are changing and try to be one of those people to fit in there. When I first started in the business, [there were] a lot of the excuses, a lot of the feedback in the industry—we can't find any black folks who can speak English, who can speak the language. We can't find anyone who is articulate. We can't find any of this, we can't find that. We'd like to use them but we can't find anybody who really fits. Essentially [they were] saying, we can't find anybody here who is black, but white. Lots of the younger generation, say under forty, so many more opportunities are there. I look at commercials—that's what I've done mostly over the years—there's lots of mixing and matching. You've got the young black girl who is dating the young white guy. You've got the beer spots. You've got the music, all the hip-hop, the way things have changed. Even the kids shows with young black stars. Opportunities have really opened up. I think it is a wonderful thing. I stay positive about it because hopefully I tell all these kids, you're going to be in another part, you're going to need a grandfather, you're going to need an uncle, you're going to need this, need that. These young kids, some of them are making movies, they're filmmakers, they're writers. And there is lots of stuff that's happening that was not happening in the past. If you can do it, if you can deliver the goods, it may be a little rough with the racial stuff, but the possibility is there.

Amy Hill: I had every obstacle. I don't look Asian enough for the Asian parts. I don't look Caucasian enough for Caucasian stuff. I'm too fat, I'm not fat enough. I'm too tall. Everything that could be possibly wrong with me being successful in this business, I own all of that. For me there was no other choice. I thought, if I have to I'll just perform on my front porch because this is what I love to do. I never quit; there were times when I felt despair, but in life I think that is only natural. I tell young Asian American actors all the time if they focus on the obstacles they are going to destroy themselves. They have to focus on their passion. They have to feel as though they have a right to be there. Not just be a good businessperson, which is important as well, but to focus on being good. Not focus on the end product. You have to suck up your ego and do the mailroom cliché. You got to go in and start at the bottom. I see a lot of young actors working so hard and not letting their egos get in the way. Even now I just costarred in two movies and I'm still getting called in for two lines.

Erick Avari: When I came to Hollywood [race] really started to play a strong part and it started quite by accident. When I first came here I was playing generic roles, Doctor Smith, Mr. Adams. I would get more of the Egyptian roles, the terrorist roles, and this was pre-9/11. I didn't play that many Indian roles so much as Middle Eastern; I fit much more into that category. It got my foot in the door. It provided a living. I got to know more people, more casting directors—it was a big help in that sense. It was always a question of doing an accent. I started to build that repertoire, it was primarily my bread and butter. Post-9/11 I felt the environment changed overnight. It didn't matter where you were from, it mattered where you looked like you were from. I made a decision that unless it was something special I'm not going to do any accents. To me it felt much more important to establish myself as an American actor, not one of those convenient actors who could do different accents. I feel there is a carryover of how people see you. I'm talking of people on the street.

Anne DeSalvo: You have to be very flexible. It's hard. I used to be offered so many things; now I have to read for everything, even episodic television. You have to stay authentic to who you are and not let your ego get crazy because so much of it is out of your control. I've learned that I am not my work. That took some real doing. Now my life is so full with so many things, but acting is still my first love. The roles are fewer so you think to yourself, how can I stay creative? I love all aspects of the business. So I tried my hand at writing and wrote *Women Without Implants*. I took a film course with Jim Pasternak on how to direct. I started hanging around the camera a lot more as I got older, listening—what this two-shot is here. Listening, picking it up because I knew I had an interest in it. When I worked with Diane Keaton on *Unsung Heroes*, she said, "You should really start thinking [about directing] because there is going to come a time when the roles get fewer and fewer." I admired what she was doing. Jim [Pasternak] said, "You should write something." I said, "No I don't write." He said, "No, Anne, you're funny—write something." So I wrote a scene—then an end scene and a beginning scene and I wrote the middle; then I shot it.

Vic Polizos: I have had to persevere more in the last few years than I did in the early days. I had all the energy and stuff when I was young. Nothing was going to stop you, but of course something does. The last few years when it has been slower it has been harder to persevere. You have to keep your eyes on the prize. It's there, it is there for all of us still. It becomes harder because you have to raise a family and come up with a certain amount of money each week. You also have to maintain your self-esteem. Which is really, really hard when it means as much to you.

Klea Scott: It's hard because casting is about putting you in a box. Stereotyping you. For me because I am mixed race—I speak French. And though I don't speak Spanish, I look like I speak Spanish. When I speak as Klea, I've been told I have a different kind of a lilt, a dialect that sometimes comes out, which is not urban black American. Which in the casting world is confusing. I don't think people get that I am an actor. This is Klea talking to you right now, if you're casting me off of myself. It's different than asking me—here's a script, and asking me to play a character from the South, or they're from England, or they are from inner-city Chicago. That's part of what I do as an actor. What I found is in the world of theater, casting directors and directors have a bigger imagination. Nobody seems to have any problem casting a black woman in any of these roles. [Klea was cast as Creon in *Antigone*, Duchess in *The Revenger's Tragedy*, and multiple roles in *History of American Film* in theater school]. I walk into a film and TV casting session, it was very specific. We need her to be dark-skinned, we don't want to wonder what race she is. "Why don't you speak Spanish? You look like you speak Spanish." It's just much more limiting and immediate. It's different in theater. I'm able to express myself in a much broader range.

Steve Vinovich: About three or four years ago I all of a sudden had eight months when I didn't work. I went to one of my fellow actors and I was really bummed and I said, "I haven't worked in eight months. I never had this happen to me before." The guy looked at me and [said], "You never had that happen before?" I realized I am one of the lucky ones; it happens more often than not. It's hard, it's very hard, and it makes you crazy. You've got to find something to fill the time with. Larry Moss, a wonderful acting teacher, he is all about that. Making something happen for yourself. Writing for yourself. Either take a class, do something. Keep it going because you've got to keep your instrument going—a pianist practices every day—actors wait around, waiting for the phone to ring.

Lupe Ontiveros: I have a friend that says—he's Latino, very successful little actor—"I don't know why they always ask me about Latino issues. The stereotypes, and have Latinos made it? I don't have a problem with it. I've always worked." I say to him, "Just because you don't have a problem doesn't mean the problem doesn't exist. You are confronting attitudes, issues that precede you before you ever walk in there." There is an attitude in Hollywood that prevails and continues to prevail in the worst possible way because nobody knows who we are. Nobody wants to know the indigenous, the Native American. Nobody really wants to know the Asian Pacific. Nobody wants to know the Latino. The African American has made his presence very aware. As Latinos we are gaining a great deal of economic power, buying power. Why the studios refuse to create the shows that really portray us as we really are. We are a vast array of stories at every level, every social echelon. You cannot ignore the reality that surrounds you. The best thing I would recommend to young actors is write your own, create your own material. The hell with Hollywood.

Amy Aquino: Age is a problem no matter what. You get older, there are fewer jobs. I've always been a character [actor] and I'll always be a character. As you get older, there are more character jobs than straight jobs for women. The only noncharacter jobs basically are for very young women or very famous beautiful women who are a little bit older. So I haven't had as serious transitional problems as women who were ingenues or young leading women.

Michael Paul Chan: Look at all the Asian American actors in Holly-wood that came before you. Look at what they did, look at what their jour-ney was. Know all there is to know about all the Asian minorities because that's what you're going to get. Soon as you get on that screen, the majority of this country is going to say, "Oh, there's the Asian guy." You have a responsibility to have some sort of dignity. Like it or not, you are a voice of your people. There were a lot of Chinese American actors—I used to cringe, until I heard their stories. A writer that got me into acting did an oral history of all the Chinese American actors [Benson Fong, Keye Luke, Victor Sen Young]—the kinds of shackles that were strapped on them before they could act. Things they could do in a scene, they couldn't [do because of restrictions on interpersonal relationships]. They wanted to touch someone, look at someone in the eye, a lot of little things they had to skip around. Things they wanted to say, they had to do in subtle ways. Any little part I get I've always tried to find some sort of dignity to whatever I'm doing. Especially playing lots of villains. Show some sense of humor.

Anne-Marie Johnson: The industry likes to stereotype. They also like to pigeonhole. Performers who are of color, especially African Americans and Latinos, really fall in this horrific gray-matter hole that if you're not African American enough, you are not going to be considered for a lot of roles. This industry is all about visual identification. I happen to be a fair-skinned African American woman and so I'm not asked to audition for a significant number of roles. I also had to say no to a lot of roles that I found insulting, quite stereotypical, that did absolutely nothing to move the African American culture. There was a line in *Hollywood Shuffle*, "There's always a job at the post office." I really adhere to that. I didn't want to sell myself or my community out short just to make a living.

Debra Monk: The women who are young ingenues, when they turn older it's always a difficult time for them. I was never an ingenue even when I was in my late twenties. I had the opportunity to play lots of parts. I always looked older so I was playing forty-year-olds when I was thirty. It's always given me the opportunity to do a lot of work. I find them to be funny great parts, parts that you can get your teeth into. It has totally helped me to have a long career. I always play the mother, the aunt, and I guess I'm getting into grandmothers now. For me it's just been more fun. I don't think I could stand the pressure of being an ingenue. I think it gets harder when you get older. The hard thing right now is there were always these wonderful supporting parts in films and television that I always had a shot at. Now a lot of Oscar winners are now interested in these parts. So we have a lot of competition with names—that's the hardest part about being a character actress now. Another thing about being a character actress is eventually a lot of them drop out of the business; I'm still here. You have to stay and hopefully those parts will come up.

Emily Kuroda: It is getting a little better, but it is still limited. A lot of it is still often stereotypical. But don't sell out to what is written on the page. Many, many times I've said, "No, I'm not going to do it that way." Because you have got to be proud of who you are. People are not aware— simply don't know—and many times if you just tell them, "I disagree with you. Can I do it this way?" Or "I'll do it this way," and have a dialogue. Most of the time it works out for the better.

Julio Oscar Mechoso: Let's say they want a young, blond, blue-eyed, good-looking, tall, handsome guy. And you are just like that. You have to be aware there are going to be another fifty guys that look like you. Yes, there are more roles out there if you belong to the majority ethnic and controlling group. I think that is a fact in every culture. But it is a competition anyway. I've always had faith if you are really that good and really meant to act—that is your true calling—ain't nobody going to get in your way. You're going to work—doing what, I don't know, but you're going to work. They are going to see that, there are people out there looking [at] that. There are very few Spanish roles written out there. But for Cuban Americans it's even smaller. No matter what, brother, no matter what, no matter who you are, there are going to be people out there competing against you.

April Grace: The things that are fantastic to me have to do specifically with the fact that I have faith. That I am able to inspire a little girl or boy, no matter what color they are, that is the payoff. As a black woman telling stories to people who are not black people and have them hear me and understand me. There is nothing more fantastic. It doesn't happen as often as I would like to see it happen, but it is getting much, much better. My black sisters who are out there auditioning—and have children of their own—don't want to play a crack whore, again. They don't want to play a bad single mother, again. I have a lot of sister friends who say yes to roles [so as to support their family] that normally they would not. For those of us like me who don't have children and only have to worry about taking care of themselves, it would behoove us to say no to those roles. To make choices and be confident in that.

Juanita Jennings: I have been doing this for a while now and I've seen quite a few changes. People before me opened the door a bit. I've opened the door a bit and that's just the way it goes. If I were to dwell on being black or being a woman, I wouldn't do anything. That's not my focus in life. I am a human being. Everything has its limitations. I'm not saying there aren't areas in the business that need to be dealt with. But all in all, I think things are moving along. I'm so happy to see today's generation have the opportunities that were not available to me when I started. I'm like, wow! I embrace that. There was an actress who passed away, quite a few years [ago] now, Rosalind Cash. When I met her years ago, she was just a blessing to me. It didn't matter that she was younger than I am, she embraced me. She said, "Go girl, you're wonderful, go, go, go." And that's how I feel. "Go, go, go, young people. Go, go, go. Don't forget me if there's an older character." [*laughs*] I think it's all good, I really do. My son has, I don't know what he is going to end up doing, but he has done some theater. Been to Edinburgh [Theater Festival], worked in his high school, done a lot of theater. If this is what he wants to do, I think there's some opportunities for him. It's what he makes of it. I think if you want to dwell on being black, dwell on being this, dwell on being that, then that's your problem. We have choices as actors. There's a lot of things that have been written that are. . . demeaning, not just by white writers, but by black writers as well. I feel that it is my prerogative to say to my agent, no, I'm going to pass on that. Even if I have to go and waitress or whatever. I'd rather pass on something that I don't feel right in my heart about. Even if it's a lead because I have to live with *me*.

CHAPTER NINE

Living a Life as an Actor

There is great nobility in being an actor. As actors we creatively express the human condition. This is a vital part of the society we live in. We have the capacity to entertain and inform an audience. That is why groups of people are eager to gather into a darkened theater or sit in front of their television sets and are willing to suspend reality, so as to be transported to another place and time and be entertained. Actors who are empowered as storytellers, truthfully acting out imaginary circumstances, have a unique ability to affect people's lives with humor and passion. That is what draws us to our work. It is the business aspect of having a career as a working actor that is most difficult. Anyone who has ever led the life of a working actor will tell you how demanding a lifestyle it is. There is the constant job insecurity and the competition among so many other talented individuals at every audition. Talent, good looks, and perseverance will not guarantee you success. Actors can get so caught up in the themselves and their careers that they may lose perspective of the importance of living a full life. This profession can wear on your self-esteem and sense of self-worth. There are no words to describe what it is like to suffer the heartbreak all actors must go through, until you experience it for yourself. Almost every actor interviewed for this book will tell you that if there is anything else in the world that you are better suited to than being an actor, then do that. This is not an occupation for everyone. It is constantly demanding younger, prettier, more talented people. Today's favorite is tomorrow's leftover. One good actor can be replaced by another. Why then, with so much that is beyond our control, would anyone want to lead the life of a working actor? There must be something about acting that becomes so addictive that you are willing to sacrifice so much to pursue your passion.

As actors we are the heroes in our own mythical journeys. We have chosen a path where we are constantly in search of meaning. And we have this wonderful gift that we want to share. This profession, like so few others, demands that we express ourselves in our work. We dip into the well of who we are and can move an audience to tears or make them laugh uproariously. We find strength in exposing our vulnerabilities, which audiences can identify with. Actors use their entire being in their work. Affecting an audience is one of the most rewarding aspects of being an actor. This emotional truth creates a powerful bond with an audience. Actors have the forum to create social change by who they are and by the characters they create on stage and in film and television.

To be an actor is to become a life learner. For every role they play, actors get to discover a new part of themselves in their work. Each character challenges us to find out more about how we operate as human beings. We get to experience physical behavior and new relationships, depending on the demands of the material. When doing background research for a part that takes place during another period in history, actors discover another world from the one in which they currently live. Good, hardworking actors are some of the most educated people I know. They are constantly questioning the hows and whys of life. One of the treasures of being on location during filming is having the opportunity to meet with the local population and learn more about how these individuals live. Many times there will be specialists in a particular field, depending on the written material, who will inform you of the intricacies of the period. Interesting and inquisitive actors are great observers of human behavior. We earn our own master's degree in psychology as we develop a greater understanding of ourselves and the world that we are a part of.

To be an actor is to be part of a collaboration. It is exciting to be part of this process with so many other creative individuals. To be able to express ourselves with beautifully written words from a talented writer is a gift. We become energized as a team of fellow artists create a costume for us, style our hair and makeup, design and light a set, all with the intention of helping us tell the story. We get to be inspired by an imaginative director who creates trust and risk taking on the set. Actors flourish in these settings. When all these elements come together, the creative instincts take over and there comes a heightened sense of reality when performing. We connect with our fellow actors in the moment. We bond with the audience, producing this actor "high," where we are all breathing together as if we are one. Moments like this are what keep us coming back to the work time and time again.

One of the best parts of being a working actor, when you are fortunate to be able to financially support yourself, is the freedom you have with your time. You can take classes to expand your horizons, volunteer, or give back to your community in some way. It is your responsibility to maintain your self-discipline while seeking balance in your life and keeping creative. When starting out as a young actor, trying to create a career can become all-consuming. It seems to represent everything of who you are, and understandably so. Once you begin to establish yourself as an actor you begin to appreciate that this is a profession. You go to work like everyone else does. You perform your job as well as you possibly can and then you go home. As you mature you begin to realize you must continue to develop your life outside of the profession. Form meaningful relationships, start a family if so desired, without waiting until the big *when* ever happens. (*When* I become famous and make so much money, then I will think about those things.) Every older, experienced person will tell you life goes by quickly. It doesn't seem that way when you are young, but it does. I encourage you not to miss out on living your life, for you won't get this time back.

An important question an actor has to ask herself is if she wants to attempt a professional career in New York or Los Angeles. That becomes a personal decision based on what type of career you envision for yourself and the kind of lifestyle you are most suited for. When weighing these options, know that neither city will have everything you may want. Some aspiring actors want to have a career in the theater while others have always dreamed of acting in film. This will help them gravitate to the New York stage or to a Hollywood studio. If you have a network of friends who have preceded you to either coast, speak with them about their experiences. Ask yourself, Am I more of a city person or a suburbanite? Do I want to travel by subway or drive a car? Do I enjoy the energy of New York or the more laid-back feeling of being in Los Angeles? I started my career in New York and now reside in Los Angeles, so I can tell you some of the pros and cons of both places.

In New York there seems to be a greater respect for actors and their commitment to the stage. People in the industry come to the theater and support your work. Whether you start up your own acting company or join an established theater organization or travel the country doing regional theater, there is a community of like-minded actors who have similar goals and interests. There is an energy and excitement you can feel in New York when just walking the streets, going from one place to the next. Cultural opportunities, which are an important part of an actor's educational growth, are everywhere. If you are going to be an actor, you have to study the craft of acting, and New York has its share of excellent acting teachers and theater programs. Going to Broadway, Off, and Off Off Broadway and watching other actors work will expand your insight into good stage acting as well as help you decide whom to study with. An actor working on the stage can be noticed by a casting director or talent agent more often in New York. I supported myself working in the theater in New York by acting in commercials, industrial films, and occasional soap operas. In addition, New York City is made up of multiple economic industries beyond the acting profession. That makes it easier to escape from the relentlessness of the career and take in other life experiences.

As everyone knows, New York is a tremendously expensive place in which to live. Housing is difficult to find for the amount of money you can afford when starting out. The pace of the city is hectic twenty-four hours a day, which for some is a blessing and for others, a curse. There is a constant ruggedness to the quality of life that can become wearing. This is made even tougher when you are not earning enough money to escape from it all. Though it is very admirable to be committed to acting work on the stage, salaries can for the most part be very low. Unless you earn Broadway-star wages, it is nearly impossible to earn your living as a stage actor. Though there are more and more television and film opportunities being created in New York, they are not anywhere near as plentiful as they are in Los Angeles. Almost every actor I know has at one time or another made the trek to Los Angeles for television pilot season.

First and foremost, Los Angeles has more higher-paying acting opportunities in film and television than anywhere else. That is why there are so many actors competing for work and living here. Of the circle of actors I interviewed for this book, the vast majority of them started their careers in New York but eventually established their base in Los Angeles for that reason. Earning a living in film and television has afforded these working actors a comfortable lifestyle they would not have had by working in the theater. Being a working actor in Los Angeles and creating more of name for themselves gives them the opportunity to work in the theater, which they weren't able to afford in the past. At one time I thought an actor had to start in New York for theatrical training, but after having taught and acted here in Los Angeles all these years, I don't think that is necessarily true anymore. Los Angeles has many wonderful acting teachers. There are scores of theater companies producing work for actors to perform in. There is as interesting acting work on stage in L.A. as there is in New York, though it is not as prevalent. In addition, there is a vibrant independent film world casting out of L.A., professionally and through the numerous film schools in the area. Commercial wok, once the domain of New York, is now more equally distributed between there and Los Angeles. It is also more affordable to live in the L.A. area when getting started, and the temperate weather creates an easier lifestyle.

With so many more acting opportunities in film and television come so many more actors competing for work. The term *cattle call* will take on a greater meaning when signing in at an audition in L.A. With so many actors to choose from, there seems to be less respect for the individual artist. It is harder to get a casting director or talent agent to come and see your stage work. Los Angeles can be called a one-industry town. Everyone seems to be in the biz or be aspiring to break into it, which makes it harder to escape the profession. If you allow it to, the sheer distance of the city can make you feel isolated. It is not as convenient to walk to a museum or a show; you usually have to get into your car and drive for a period of time.

My area of expertise has been in creating and maintaining an acting career on either coast. Any actor who wishes to break into film and television and still wants the opportunity to work in the theater will eventually have to migrate to New York or Los Angeles. Having said that, there are other great cities in the United States such as Chicago, Seattle, Boston, Minneapolis, Atlanta, and Dallas that have vibrant acting communities. Along with established regional theaters throughout the country, working actors have a place to hone their craft and continue to perfom. Actors are able to supplement their acting income by working in local commercials, industrial films, and the occasional casting from the local talent pool when a film or television show casts in their community. Not everyone is cut out for the intense competition of New York and

Los Angeles. Living and performing in these alternative cities is a viable way to still have a fulfilling life as a working actor. I have had the opportunity to act in several regions of this country, where I have met scores of talented actors who once lived in either New York or Los Angeles. These performers made the personal decision to establish themselves as actors in their hometowns or cities and still pursue their acting goals.

New York and Los Angeles are exciting and challenging places in which to live. Whichever place you decide to get started in, give it time. Take root in your community as you nurture yourself to succeed. There are no quick steps to success. You have to be willing to live through what every actor struggles with in creating a career. Those who remain rooted in who they are and can adapt to change will be the talented actors who have a greater chance of living the life of a working actor.

❖ ❖ ❖ ❖

Eddie Jones: The primary thing is that you need it. You need to do it. It means a chance actually to rediscover myself. As far as I'm concerned, through the acting I get to come back to things that I know about myself, but haven't been there for a long time. I'm able to express emotionally, especially. It attracted me. It attracted me because within that context you were able to express yourself. To walk into new situations and to learn things. To learn things about yourself that you didn't know. You turn a corner in a play sometimes and all of a sudden you are in another world. And it's true, you have never been there before and the hair on the back of your neck goes up. You share that with the audience; it's astounding at times. It doesn't happen that often. That makes the whole trip worthwhile. Aside from the gratification from doing a good job, in the strictest sense, it's very educational. There are so many situations you run into, so many things you have to research, to track down. Who's this guy, what's he play, what were the times like? What kind of shoes did he wear, did he have a nail file in his pocket? . . . I have found it to be very frustrating, but most of the times quite rewarding. I think once you have an identification as an actor, it doesn't preclude anything else, when you think of yourself as an actor. I know people, friends that probably haven't worked in five or six years, ten years. They are actors, it doesn't matter.

Lauren Tom: I'm really glad I didn't go to L.A. right away. Now that I have been out here for ten years, I know I wouldn't have been ready. You really need to be more grounded out here than you have to be in New York. I found the difference that in New York I felt that they were looking for the essence of who I was for a part. I found it to be so visual out here. If you have talent, it is sort of icing on the cake. Some people can make a big splash but if you don't have the chops, it probably won't last. I found the casting people were ready to gobble me up because I was new and young. They hadn't seen me before but I didn't think that my theater credits meant all that much to the casting people out here [L.A.]. I kind of got that hint that it was going to be about the visual and the newness.

John Rothman: The decision to stay in New York and to base a career here as opposed to Hollywood was a concern. There is clearly more work out there, more opportunities. As a very wise fellow said to me, "An actor's life is a life of opportunities." Which is actually a very useful thing to remember. When you don't get this job, that job, the next opportunity is coming. There are more opportunities in film and television in California. Film and television is where you can make a living in this business. It is so rare that it is almost unheard of to make what you consider a middle-class living [in the theater]. To make the kind of living to live in New York or Los Angeles in the theater. It almost cannot be done. A Broadway star, I suppose, but how many? Yes, there are people who have done it, but it better be a musical and it's going to be exceptional. The way you do it in New York is by doing commercials, doing voice-overs. It supports working in the theater. That's harder to do now. It used to be all the commercial business was here. In the last ten years, however, I've had to have a Los Angeles component in my career. I spend time there—pilot season, hoping to get work on a series. I did a New York series that I got in L.A. If I was in New York I probably wouldn't have gotten the job. Being perceived as a New York actor is an advantage when you're in L.A. It's a balancing act.

Nike Doukas: I grew up on the East Coast, and New York doesn't have the allure for me that it does for a lot of people. I didn't like living in New York, how expensive it was to live, I hate the weather out there—I'm not a winter person. For me I always have to have a place to live that I like. I love the West Coast. The minute I came out here, I felt this is where I belong, so I wanted to be in L.A. I felt like it was still hard to get work as an actor in New York on stage. Everyone told me I was a New York actor—people don't appreciate you in L.A. I felt if I could get a TV series, then I could do a play in New York. I always felt very strongly that I am not in this to do [Equity] waiver theater. I'm in this to make a living. That's my job.

Armin Shimerman: Young actors must really look at themselves, look deep in their hearts, and say, "Which medium do I want to perform in?" Really be honest with yourself. If it is film and TV, then no matter where you live in the country, I would suggest you really think about moving to Los Angeles. If you were like myself and were really steeped in theater, then you have no choice but to move to New York. There are other cities where there is great theater and maybe if you are close to those cities you might want to try there first. These cities are Seattle, Minneapolis, Louisville, Chicago, Philadelphia, [Boston]—cities where there are many theaters where you can work your craft, learn to be a better actor. Learn to meet people—you can contact them later on when you move to New York or Los Angeles. Try those cities first. If you are not near any of those cities, you might as well make the big leap and go to either Los Angeles or New York.

Christine Estabrook: You're always going to be struggling as far as getting the next job. A lot of people fall into a series, and God bless them. That brings it own problems. You are in a series for a long time, you're hoping to God the writers will write for you because if they don't, your life is unbearable. You have to seek doing your art elsewhere. You have to work little projects for yourself, get into a theater. You have to really enjoy what's enjoyable because it's a long life. [*laughs*]

Erick Avari: My wife was an actress in New York and her work was primarily in New York. She did a lot of soaps, started a theater company in New York. She was rooted in New York and, at the time, a lot of my work—certainly the better-paying work—was out in the regions. I'd find myself in Minneapolis, Cleveland, Texas, all over the country for months at a time. It was difficult, which is why we don't have kids today. That was one of the sacrifices that we talked about and made. We sat and talked about it and said, "What do we want more?" It was clear to both of us that we really wanted to pursue our careers. We would have loved to have had kids, [but] it was just not feasible.

Carol Potter: I think the attitude [that actors are disposable] in Los Angeles is much worse than in New York. The other thing worse than that in Los Angeles is the attitude about money. In Los Angeles there is a lot less respect accorded the work if you're not making money at it. I think in New York, people are very aware that you can spend your life in the theater and have an incredibly productive career. You can be an amazingly talented actor and be constantly challenged in your work and not make a lot of money. There was respect for that choice. I don't think there is as much respect for that choice on this side of the world.

Andrew Prine: Most young actors can't hear this any more than I could. When it is all over, it's just about the work. Fame to some extent will follow the work. Maybe to a great extent in a few people. Thank goodness it wasn't more, it might have destroyed some of us. It might have been too much, it destroys people too. We don't remember those people as well. It is hard to handle. You think you want these things, but once you get them, they start wearing. It is not substantial; it doesn't lead to happiness. You get money, thank goodness; you can live, good—that's a wonderful thing for any profession—but beyond that it is baloney, absolute baloney.

Magda Harout: To be an actor is to be alive, to live, that's me. To experience. If you're lucky you get to transfer that experience to your audience. The greatest joy is to be doing something in front of an audience and having them react the way you want them to react. That is the joy. You're reaching out and touching people and they're touching you back. That's the reward you get. Whether your audience is thousands and thousands, or on a bad day, five people in the audience, when the cast outnumbers the audience. The most uplifting and wonderful thing is to be able to reach people, touch them, and have them touch you. You're alive, you're a person, you're in the world, and the world is full of wonderful people as well as some terrible people. But you experience it all. And if you don't experience everything, good, bad, and indifferent, you're not living. You're just not living. I don't care what stage an actor is at, they are living the fullest in that time period.

Carol Potter: The hardest thing for me has always been having to drop everything and go do what you have to do. You have your day planned, and the night before you get an audition. Or the night before you get a call for a job. Or the night before they call you, they are switching the scenes so they're shooting your stuff tomorrow. You get on the set and it's ten o'clock in the morning and you think you are going to be done by one and there's a snafu and you don't get done by eight or nine o'clock that night. Those are the kinds of things that drove me crazy, drove me nuts. It was very hard as a mother of a young child; I had to be very clear that I didn't know when I was going to be home. I would be home as soon as I could. I would be able to call him by a certain time if I wasn't going to be home by the time he was going to bed. That's the hardest thing for me. You're planning a vacation. I had this friend this happened to all the time; she'd plan a vacation and just before the vacation she'd go in for an audition and they'd say, "Oh, we really want you. It's this pilot; you've got to cancel your plans." So she'd cancel her plans. And nothing would happen. People don't treat you properly. They consider you disposable, dispensable. Your life is unimportant. People get so consumed by the pressure and therefore how important . . . what they are doing is. And how everybody else should fall by the wayside. That is very hard to deal with.

Emily Kuroda: Actors are some of the most incredibly talented people I have ever met. Working with them has helped me as a human being— I've grown. I am so fortunate to be in this community of actors, directors, writers. It feeds my soul. It is like reading a book. When you read a book you feel like you have gone there. Acting enabled me to go to places I would have never been able to go to before. When I did a film about geishas in Japan, I was able to go into that house. See how they live, how they work, talk to them and really understand them by getting to know them for a number of weeks. I did another movie about women in prison and we got to go to many of the prisons in California and talk with the inmates, spend the day with them. That was something that hit me to the core. I can't say it in words, but it has become a part of me.

Gregory Itzin: I always felt, what is it that I can do, what difference can I make? [Acting] wasn't a hard thing to do, I got strokes for it. I came to a crossroads when I got older; insecurities began to creep in. I needed to find a reason—I got tired of doing acting, tired of the business. I did a lot of theater, but at the same time the patina started to go off of the golden bowl. I had to reassess things. I started looking at what it was we did. I thought of looking at it in a more spiritual fashion. I thought, this is what I do in the world. I have been blessed in a way with a gift—everybody has a gift—this is my gift. I do this pretty darn well. I choose what I want to do when I do theater and say, "What is the gift of this play?" It is not that I'm a religious person, but I do believe we are all on a journey and this is what mine is.

Vic Polizos: I'm from Montgomery, Alabama, and years ago a guy came up to me who had done a few extra roles, shot in Montgomery. He said, "Boy, I wish I had your life. The actor's life, that's the life. You sit around and get to act and get paid a lot of money." He said, "That's the life I want. You sleep late, you go to bed late, do whatever you want to." I told him, "You don't know what you're are talking about. You don't have a clue." My life is not a vacation. I would love to work five days a week, eight hours a day. Making a lot of money all the time. I might make a good check once every two or three months. Maybe twice a month if I'm lucky. That's when I'm really working well. The rest of the time you are waiting. And when you do get the opportunity, you go in there and put yourself in front of people who either think you are too tall, too fat, or talk too slow, or they have no idea what they want. You try and have people tell you *no* five time a week. No, we don't like you. No, we don't want to see you again. No, we don't like what you did. No, we don't like what you look like. I think the life of the actor is really hard, emotionally certainly. Physically you sleep late, but that's because you are depressed.

Amy Aquino: When I was setting out on this path, I said if I was going to do mediocre work, mediocre jobs, then I'll just do something else. While I've been very lucky because I've been involved with really wonderful things, I haven't been the star of very much. I've been able to let go of the idea of needing to be a big star. I am happy with the fact that I seemed to [have] been able to affect some people's lives. That's a good thing, that's enough. I was just finishing a movie and I had to fly out to L.A. to audition for *LA Law* as a regular. My mother said to me, "You're going to make it, I just know it." I said, "You know what, Mom, just for the record, for the sake of argument, I've made it. OK! I'm supporting myself as an actor, I have a good agent, I've got a good future, I'm OK, I'm there."

James Rebhorn: To me L.A. is a one-industry type of a town and the industry is entertainment. Pretend is pretense, hype. Whenever I've been out there, I find it stifling. Doubly troubling is it's deceptively beautiful. For me that was not the place for me to develop a career or a life as a professional actor. It might be fine to live there, but not as an actor. Despite the fact that I have always almost felt uncomfortable in New York because it is a city you can never turn off, I find it much more stimulating. The diversity of it provides much more fodder for my imagination. I like the fact that I can walk down a couple of blocks in New York City and see millions of different body types, nationalities, different ethnic heritages, different racial makeups—that I love. I came into this business in the theater and I still value my experience with the theater and still want to keep working in the theater. Theater is more important here [in New York] ultimately than it is in Los Angeles.

Willie C. Carpenter: From where I am now from where I was, I couldn't have planned it. It just evolved into something that I'm pretty pleased with. I had no idea what direction it was going in. You always fantasize about doing a little better—I'm nowhere near where I'd like to be. When you see your friends and suddenly their careers take off, it is inspiring. I'm still inspired. I still have the fantasy of hitting a big paycheck. The fame has never been the important thing with four children. I have often said yes to jobs that if I were single I would have said no. My goal is to raise a family, to earn a living—that's foremost. A lot of people come into the business because they love acting. I do too, but I had to earn money, I had to earn a living, and I found out I was good at this. Also if you're lucky, they pay you a lot of money, the sky was the limit.

Anne DeSalvo: The stage is God in New York. The respect for stage in New York is tremendous. The respect for the actor, the respect for the playwright is something I greatly miss here [L.A.]. Not to denigrate Los Angeles because there are a lot of terrific people out here—directors, writers, and so on. You do get into the business out here in so many different ways. You go on *American Idol*, then you're starring in a movie. In New York it is a little bit more legitimate. Also the stage there—you can reinvent yourself on the stage. Here you do plays and no one comes. It's more, what is your TV-Q [TV popularity rating quotient]? Then again, New York wants television and film stars to bring in money for the box office. You have to have a balance.

H. Richard Greene: I chose not to live in the regional theater circuit but to move to New York and then L.A. I wanted to be in the most intense, demanding, and rewarding environment. I welcomed that.

Shakespeare went to London. We have to go to the center, the heart of it. Throw ourselves into it. That's how you test yourself. If you really want to do this, you should welcome this thrilling, scary opportunity.

Sheila Kelley: I think the life of the working actor is erratic. It depends on what you make it. If you choose to be a victim, if you choose to be the one who needs to be accepted, you will probably have a miserable existence. Going from job to job—we tend to surf each job—we go up with each job we get and we come down when we don't get another one. We wait for it to come out and we don't get accepted and we kind of crash; we go to another audition and come up the wave and we go down the wave—it is a very difficult and emotionally taxing way to live.

Armin Shimerman: The life of an actor is primarily [one of] quiet desperation, sometimes not so quiet. One, there is always the financial. Two, I don't care who you are—Tom Hanks or whoever—there is always the question of where your next job is coming from. More importantly because we are always at everyone's beck and call, you're never really secure in your own work. You never know if it is good enough. That insecurity lives with you constantly. What an actor needs to have is a very large ego to withstand all those questions, those doubts that come from every possible place, pinging upon your mental security. You need to be able to somehow . . . say, I can deal with this. I am going to have doubts, I am going to have insecurities, but I am going to bounce back. If you can't do that, you really must get another profession because it will drive you crazy. The truth of the matter is I know that 80 percent can't live with that. I know actors who are relatively successful and have no financial problems who are plagued by the idea that they don't know when the next job is coming and if they are any good. We only have one life and it is a tragedy that some actors, most actors, have to live with that all their lives.

Nike Doukas: I feel sorry for people who don't feel passionate about what they do. I have not made a lot of money—I've had an outside job once for six months in my life. I feel incredibly fortunate that I can say that. I've lived like a church mouse, but I don't care. I've lived a really rich life. I've stood on a stage with two symphonies and spoken Shakespeare. I wouldn't trade that for anything. I've played roles in Shakespeare, Shaw,

Chekhov. I've originated roles with Pulitzer Prize playwrights. I think the arts are vital to our mental and emotional health. I am honored that I am able to do it. I feel like I am getting away with murder. [*laughs*]

Luck Hari: Very few people in the world outside of India have that connection to the arts that we have. All of the classical arts that we have in India—the overall purpose is a spiritual transcendental quality in the arts. People from India, we have such a deeper understanding of that. It is not an elitist activity, as often it is in a capitalist country. That's special, that's so special. To know that in your body, in your soul. It's a path thing if you feel in your heart that's what you want to do, you are often a step ahead with your connection to the arts. As [Friedrich] Nietzsche said, "The arts are the saving sorceress of our species."

Ashley Gardner: It's being creative, having a creative life. I could have stayed at home—could have married some boy and stayed in Rocky Mount, North Carolina, and lived very comfortably. I would have died inside. I would have just died. I miss my family every day, but I'm so much happier being able to really be who I am. I wouldn't have been able to do that at home. I'm sure in this great big country of ours, there are a lot of young people who feel that way. They feel trapped by the place they grew up. Being an actor, you're creative. Your mind engages you. You're always using your imagination, you never stop using your imagination. I think in most grown-ups that becomes squashed if you're just a regular grown-up. Maybe that's it—I didn't have to completely grow up. I'm a responsible person, but I didn't have to completely grow up. That suits me just fine.

CHAPTER TEN

If I Knew Then What I Know Now, I'd...

If you asked me when I first started out on this acting journey some thirty years ago if I'd be able to accomplish all that I have, would I consider myself a success, my response would have been no. In the beginning I mistakenly believed that being a successful actor meant I had to become a famous celebrity. Nowhere did I take into account that there was a fullfilling life to lead as a working actor. But imagine someone had told me the price I would have had to pay to reach this level of success, that I would have had to face long periods of unemployment and financial insecurity, and if that wasn't enough, that I would also have had to confront my fears and learn how to handle the constant rejection and heartbreak that comes with this profession. Knowing what I know now, and the sacrifices I would have to make, would I have still headed down this road? My answer would be an unequivocal yes! When I was a young man I needed to act. With so much emotional life dwelling up inside of me, I needed to find an outlet where I could express myself. Acting became my salvation. It afforded me the opportunity to merge the different parts of who I am with the roles that I was playing in a creative way. It led me to feel whole as a human being. As this process unfolded, I discovered that my fellow actors had similar feelings that needed to be expressed. I then felt like I belonged to the family of actors. The colleagues I trained with, my contemporaries whom I have performed with, and the acting students who have studied with me are all willing to fight the good fight, just so we might have the opportunity to act. I have tremendous admiration for anyone who is willing to take on this challenge and give it his or her all.

We never want to live with "What if?" As actors we want to know that we gave it our best shot. If it is meant to be, then it will happen. Perhaps not the way you dreamed it would, but hopefully there will be enough triumphs that you'll be able to say you are successful. What you don't want is to live with the regret that you either didn't try to become an actor at all or attempted your career halfheartedly. When the reward is no longer worth the struggle, you'll be able to move on to do something else with your life. You'll know in your heart of hearts that you did everything in your power to succeed. Somewhere along the line almost every actor I know has had to face this dilemma. When you set realistic and timely goals for yourself, you then can stop to evaluate how far you have come and whether or not you should continue.

If I had to do it all over again, would I do anything differently? One way to respond is to say if I made a different choice somewhere along the line, then perhaps I wouldn't end up where I am now. There are things that I recognize now that I wish I had a greater understanding of how to handle at the time. But that is what experience teaches us. When proposing this question to the actors I interviewed, I framed it in two ways: Would you share your wisdom and offer advice to anyone who is considering becoming an actor? Or if you knew then what you know now, would you have gone about a part of this process in a different way? Here then are *fifty-one tips* of shared experience and advice, some of which have been previously mentioned in the book but bear repeating. Come back to this page when you can use some needed encouragement.

Most importantly, follow your passion, for without it, you are nothing as an actor.

Know that you have a gift to share and be gentle with yourself.

Develop your craft of acting so that you have a proven way of working; living off your instincts will take you only so far.

Become connected to your inner life.

Maintain your sense of humor so as not to take yourself too seriously.

Persevere.

Invest in yourself.

Continue to grow as an artist by expanding your creative horizons.

Preparation is vital.

Don't become complacent when you begin working on a steady basis.

Be gracious and generous when things go your way.

Every career has its share of ups and downs.

When you have the opportunity to work on a regular basis, ride it out as long as possible—it won't last forever.

Make strong choices.

This is not brain surgery. No one's life is at stake.

You are an independent contractor. Keep a good record of pay stubs and time sheets.

Save your money! I guarantee you will need it sometime during your career.

Write something to act in.

Join a group of like-minded actors so you have friends to network with and be mutually supportive of.

It's a numbers game, so don't take it personally.

You don't have to make excuses for what you haven't done. It's what you are going to do that counts.

Learn how to care less about caring.

Waiting by the telephone will make you crazy.

It's selection, not rejection.

Those that take no for an answer will not succeed.

The acting profession is a marathon, not a sprint.

Everyone auditions poorly at times.

Maintain artistic integrity in yourself and your work.

Show humility.

Keep a balanced life.

Exercise.

Have outside interests and hobbies that feed you.

Life goes by quickly, so give it everything you've got. You won't get this time back.

Be willing not to know and be open to asking questions.

Taking risks demands courage. Take your fear in stride.

Breathe.

Create your own work.

Volunteer.

Remain optimistic and stay away from cynicism.

Seek out the truth.

Use your imagination.

Stay in touch with your childlike sense of wonderment and play.

Set realistic goals for yourself. Write them down.

If you are happy doing something else, then do that.

Maintain self-discipline.

Let go of the results.

Stay in the moment.

Return to the stage to keep your instrument alive.

There are no shortcuts to success.

Find nobility in the struggle.

Act!

❖   ❖   ❖   ❖

Randle Mell: Young actors have a lot of ideas about what it is to be an actor. They have a lot of ideas about what it is to be successful. What it is to be famous. I think they lose touch sometimes with what brought them to this place to begin with, which was a visceral experience of acting. Of saying beautiful or intelligent words. Of expressing their emotions. What I encourage young actors to do is follow their instincts. If they read a play that they respond to on an emotional or intellectual level, try to do it. Look for places to work, to do the kind of work you are interested in doing, whether it's a play or a film. Do student films with people at a film institute. Do the work without trying to place too much expectation on it. Is this going to make me successful? Is this going to lead to where I think I want to go? To pay more attention to the instinctual response—does this excite me at this moment? And if it does, do it! I think we get caught up in our big plans and ideas and they can lead us astray because we lose touch with what we really respond to emotionally.

Marianne Muellerleile: One of the mistakes that young actors make is that they are not practical enough. They are very caught up in a great role, the opportunity, how many people will see them, even the paycheck.

I want them to remember that it is really just your job. You need to think long term. I don't want actors, particularly character actors, to come to a point where they think they shouldn't be accepting a one-day job in a film. I've played nuns till I'm sick to death of them. Because if they are going to have a career in TV and film, you have to also think about your residuals. You have to think long term. You could be a leading lady and at least statistically those people in those categories, even juveniles, won't have as long a career as a character person. I'd like actors to keep in mind there may be a time when their careers may slow or end. When they are looking at parts, try to look at it from a business point of view. One day at eight hundred dollars on a film that is going to be sold a gazillion times on DVDs and air forever for thirty or forty years will bring them more money than a fabulous documentary. I still want them to do the documentary, but I don't want them to turn down the one-day [job]. So many actors think they get to a level they don't have to do certain kinds of jobs. It's crazy to think that way.

Lisa Blake Richards: For young people I think it's very important that you get in a group, an acting group. Or a troupe or a company, and you do the work. That is the most important thing. You cannot sit in your house and wait for the "big break." You cannot wait by the phone. It's deadly. It doesn't create work, it creates neuroses. The way to get work is to keep busy, to keep out there, to keep working on your craft. If you don't have a network, you're just not going to work.

Hal Landon: If you have to act or life will have no meaning for you, then you should definitely try to do this. But don't give up your day job. You don't want to have that pressure of, I've got to have this job—hire me for this part or my family doesn't eat. I don't think you have to make your living as an actor to find fulfillment and satisfaction. Since I've been teaching, I've gone to see some community theater which was awfully good. I think it is possible to have your day job, do some high-quality community theater, and have a pretty fulfilling experience. You still can have an interesting life as an actor in the nonprofessional arena.

Robert Picardo: It's not a merit-rewarding career. If you are the best, you won't necessarily be rewarded accordingly. You are tied to what you look like. Your face and body is your instrument. You may think of yourself as the most beautiful human being in the world, but after five years of never getting to play opposite Julia Roberts, you've got to wake up to the fact that maybe other people don't. You may have great range, have great everything as an actor, but inevitably you are limited by whatever you are physically. I think the actors that really do well have some sort of insight into where they fit and what they can do. If you have a pretty clear idea of yourself and your talents—hopefully you have broad talents and great faith in them—but to be able to see how you fit into the industry. Direct your attack, I think that's the best way; pick accessible goals and work your ass off to get them.

Grant Albrecht: I think the number one tool you need is a sense of humor. If you have a sense of humor about yourself and this business, I think that is the greatest asset. You need gratitude—counting the blessings you have at any given time. Instead of looking at what other people have that you don't have. Finally, always nurturing your hunger to express yourself and your artistry in your own expressions. Keeping your eyes wide open to the world around you, the things that inspire you. Being very vigilant about maintaining your own point of view and perspective that is informed by a full life. Acting comes from living. Acting is reacting. If you are living your life and experiencing it fully, you're going to have something to express. That means living your life that is not just in the tiny box that is this business.

Amy Hill: I believe it is never too late to get back on that road because the gift that you have to give as a performer, as an artist, only grows as you grow older. Stay true to that path. Be diligent as an artist. Don't just focus on the business of it.

Julio Oscar Mechoso: I wouldn't recommend this to most people. You are probably bound to fail. The odds are against you to really make a living. When you make money, save. Save. You've got to save your money when you're making it because you are going to need it. As a character actor, you are hot and cold. Don't think that is what you are going to make for the rest of your life. You are only making that until they say yes, until they say no. They have all the options. Believe me, I've been in several series. They love you, they love you, they love you until the ratings come in. [*laughs*] Then it's, "We are going to have to cut back." It's a business; they have a business to run.

Miguel Sandoval: Get training. Get as much training as you can. Get as wide and varied a training as you can. It has to be on the stage because that's our only really true medium. That's the actor's medium. . . . When the lights go down, the performance starts. There's no more writer, no more director, it's just you and the audience and that's it. You have to know what that means first. Because that's really acting. This other stuff, film and TV, we have nothing to do with it. As we all know, many performances can be made great or bad depending upon the editor's whim. Get as much training as you can. Get as wide and as varied training as you can. Get trained in musical theatre. But also understand who Samuel Beckett is. Understand who some more obscure German playwrights are. Understand what performance art is. Get training in dance, get training in movement, get training in clowning and anything you can. It will only serve you in the future. And along the way at each road sign, stop and ask yourself, "Do I really have to be doing this?" If the answer is yes, by all means keep going, keep going with all your heart. If you have any doubts, answer yourself honestly.

Robin Bartlett: I think the greatest base of support that I have felt in my career is the sense you have—for all of time actors are outlaws—we have a community. No matter what level of the business you're in, that you sort of feel you're outside of society looking in. As most artists do, observing, feeding back to people what you see. We have that in common. There is a great solace in that, being a vagabond profession. It explains a lot about the personalities that go into it—why you feel more comfortable being someone else. Why you don't fit into a nine-to-five culture. The friends you make and the people you know in the business are like you. It is a great community to be part of.

Sheila Kelley: So many actors choose to wait for the jobs to come. They audition in that huge pool of auditioning actors; I just think it is [the] wrong thing to do. Whenever I got anything in the world, it is when I produced my film [*Lovers*], when I am part of the process of creating something that I believe in and have passion for. The life of the working actor can be whatever you want it to be.

Richard Fancy: When I was a young actor I knew it was so . . . important to make contact with people in the biz, like agents and stuff like that. I had no idea how to conduct myself. I think most actors don't have what people in a law firm have, which is a series of steps that they see before them. That guy is a junior partner and how he got there is that way. You say, a guy's a young actor and he became a working actor, how did that happen? How did he become [a] really well-respected working actor? There are no steps, in fact, because a lot of times people become stars right away. One of the things I discovered was in every meeting I have, I want to tell them a story. I began to see the moment as a business moment, selling them on me. I think any time you come into a room, your job is a business job. It's to tell a tale about yourself. It should be as close to the truth as possible, but you have an outcome you want done.

April Grace: I would have lived the life, as much as one can, of a successful artist. Whatever you imagine a successful artist looks like on you—whatever that walk is, whatever that glint in your eye is—I would live that every day. I would remind myself, I would be that. Not to look to be that later, but I am that now. Realize that being that has nothing to do with money. If you separate making a living from being an artist, and then walk in the way of the artist, the money will come.

Shelley Morrison: You have to love it. You have to love it. You have to love the work part of it. You have to put up with a lot of BS. You have to develop a thick skin. You're dealing with a lot of different personalities, a lot [of] egos. You have to keep your ego in check. You have to remind yourself. Have people around you that will do reality checks with you. That's a biggie. You don't want the entourage yessing everything. You have to have people saying, "Shelley, you're out of line." You just have to love it. Do it for the right reason!

H. Richard Greene: I think actors have to go out and be in the world. Have families, have experiences, have opinions about politics and art and religion and science. The more you educate yourself, the broader and deeper person you become, the more interesting you are as an actor. Unfortunately the tendency is to become insular. Actors can become very dull people if all they are thinking about is how to get the next job.

Luck Hari: It has to be the only thing you feel that you could do with your life because it is really so hard in many ways. If you feel you absolutely can't do anything else, then that's it, you were meant to be an actor, meant to be an artist. It's got to be that feeling in your soul, in your heart. When you're young you have to separate whether it's that or ego gratification. When you're younger you get so much positive feedback and that can be intoxicating. You can't see clearly whether or not if it's that or that you really have talent and it's in your soul. If that's the case, you really have to go for it. You can't deny it. I tried to, but I literally couldn't deny it was my path.

Andrew Prine: The actor and the aspiring actor has to understand that you never accept no. Because there will be another actor who is struggling just like you who is never going to accept no. That's the actor who is going to work. It is not about your talent. If you're talented that will later be proven. It is about never, never buying into the nineteen hundred times they say no. If you do you should go get another job—you should find something else to do—because the guy who is going to work is the guy you cannot shut the door on, no matter how many times you reject him and push him out the door. That's who works.

Several years ago a young reporter interviewed the late venerable actor-comedian George Burns. Here was a man who had an eight-decade career in show business while having the good fortune to live to be one hundred years old. As a child he began his career performing on the streets of New York City, singing and dancing. Eventually he successfully took his act onto the vaudeville circuit. In addition to his talented soft-shoe and singing performances, he had impeccable timing as a comedian. Burns appeared on Broadway and was summoned to Hollywood to act in motion pictures. He entertained on the radio as well as with his own television series as part of the legendary comic duo Burns and Allen. He went on to perform his act in nightclubs and on television variety shows for several more decades. He was honored with an Academy Award for best supporting actor when he was eighty years old. This legendary performer, who had played God on screen, had done and seen it all. Who better to ask for advice about being an actor? This young reporter asked Burns, who was now in his nineties, "Mr. Burns, having been in show business all your life, what advice would you give a young actor just getting started?" George Burns took a moment and puffed on his cigar. He adjusted his oversized horn-rimmed glasses. He took another, longer puff on his cigar and smacked his lips. Deep in thought, he exhaled the cigar smoke and knowingly replied, "Take your wallet on stage."

Actor's To-Do List

1. Write three pages in a stream of consciousness that describes your passion and need for acting. Use this as your foundation to draw upon when needed. As you progress along in this journey, you may want to redefine this passion so that it continues to fuel your creativity.

2. List at least five things about yourself that you believe are an honest accounting of what makes you special as an actor. It is important to know who you are and what you have to offer. This is part of the gift you have to share in your work and not the time to be modest.

3. Make a list of acting and acting-related accomplishments from the previous year. They can range from a breakthrough in acting class to a successful meeting with a casting director to booking your first job. A career is made up of small steps that accumulate over time.

4. Write out realistic goals that you want to accomplish in the coming year. Make sure to include at least one far-reaching goal that is attainable. A goal, for example, doesn't necessarily have to be getting the job (through obviously that is the eventual idea); it may be getting your first callback on a commercial within six months, joining an acting company, or creating a demo reel.

5. List at least five tasks that you have control over that you can do to achieve these goals within the next twelve months. You have more power over your career than may meet the eye. Sign up for a class, work on a new monologue, check the casting boards at the local film schools.

6. What areas do you need to improve upon to grow as an actor? Be honest and specific. Choose one to work on immediately. An actor must have the self-discipline to continue to grow as an artist. Do you need to work on your voice? Are you going into auditions with a negative attitude? Is it time to switch acting classes?

7. To maintain sanity and balance in your life, name five things that you do outside of the business that give you joy and positive reinforcement. It is hard enough maintaining a career; don't

foolishly suffer for your art. Having other physical and creative outlets will help you maintain perspective.

8. Memorize a passage from literature, a poem, or a play that you can recite that is a positive affirmation. Use it as a source of comfort and strength when you are feeling burdened by it all.

9. Write out your definition of what it means to be a success as an actor. By having a long-range vision of where you want to try to go, you can appreciate and make friends with the struggle as a meaningful part of your journey.

10. Make a list of your family and friends who are part of your support system. Include people you can count on for positive reinforcement as well as fellow artists you can rely on for honest, constructive feedback in regard to your work and career. Plan to meet with them on a recurring basis. Use part of this time together to pitch creative ideas back and forth with one another, simply listen, and most of all, have a good laugh.

Who's Who

Grant Albrecht

Grant Albrecht is a graduate of Carnegie Mellon University. His stage work includes *The Illusion*, *What the Butler Saw*, *Later Life*, *A Chorus Line*, and *The Country Wife* at such theaters as Circle in the Square, Manhattan Theater Club, the Hartford Stage, and Cleveland Playhouse. His guest-star appearances include *Law & Order*, *The Guardian*, *Just Shoot Me*, *Any Day Now*, *Malcolm in the Middle*, *CSI: NY,* and the soap operas *All My Children*, *Loving*, and *As the World Turns*. His film roles include *S.W.A.T.*, *Voodoo Dawn*, and voice work on *Cowboy Bebop: The Movie* and *Jungle Book 2*. Albrecht is a veteran of hundreds of television commercials. He has a demyelinating spinal cord condition and is a determined advocate for diversity in media for people with disabilities.

Amy Aquino has an MFA from the Yale Drama School and appeared on Broadway in *The Heidi Chronicles*. Other stage appearances include Circle Repertory, Playwrights Horizons, Williamstown Theatre Festival,

Amy Aquino

La Jolla Playhouse, Mark Taper Forum, and Geffen Theater. Aquino has been a series regular on *Madman of the People*, *Brooklyn Bridge*, and *Picket Fences*. Recurring guest-star roles include *Curb Your Enthusiasm*, *Crossing Jordan*, *ER*, *Judging Amy*, *Felicity*, and *Freaks and Geeks*. TV movie credits are *False Arrest*, *The Last to Go*, *Once in a Lifetime*, *Blood Brothers*, and *Descending Angel*. Motion picture credits include *A Lot Like Love*, *Synergy*, *White Oleander*, *Undisputed*, *Boys on the Side*, *Working Girl*, *Moonstruck*, and *Allen and Naomi*.

Erick Avari

Erick Avari appeared on Broadway in *The King and I* and *Rasputin* at Lincoln Center. Other selected credits include stage work at the New York Shakespeare Festival, Mabou Mines, South St. Theater, Guthrie Theater, and Cleveland Playhouse. Recent film credits include *Searching for Haizmann*, *Daredevil*, *Master of Disguise*, *Mr. Deeds*, *Planet of the Apes*, *The Mummy*, *The Glass House*, *Ritual*, *Independence Day*, *Stargate*, *Color of Night*, *Encino Man*, and *Kanchenjunga*. TV films are *Home Alone 4*, *Don't Drink the Water*, *True Blue*, *Treacherous Crossing*, *Hit List*, and *Casualties of Love*. Avari has had recurring episodic work on *Stargate SG-1*, *Felicity*, and *Education of Max Bickford* and has had numerous guest-star appearances.

Robin Bartlett has appeared on Broadway in *Everett Beekin*, *Yentl*, and *Sholem Aleichem*. She has performed on Off Broadway at Circle Repertory in *Reckless* and *Early Girl* and in *The Old Neighborhood* at the Geffen Playhouse in Los Angeles. Her many film credits include *City of Angels*, *Honey We Shrunk Ourselves*, *Dangerous Minds*, *Deceived*, *Regarding Henry*, *Postcards from the Edge*, *Crimes and Misdemeanors*,

Robin Bartlett

Lean on Me, Alice, Moonstruck, and *Heaven's Gate.* Bartlett has been a series regular on *The Breaks, Jonathan, It Had to Be You,* and *The Powers That Be.* She played a recurring character on *Mad About You.* Her television movie appearances include *Skokie, Playing for Time, Courage,* and *The Stalking.*

Kevin Bourland

Kevin Bourland has been featured in such films as *Volcano, Norma Jean and Marilyn, The Thing Called Love, Aspen Extreme, Sister Act, The Last Boy Scout, Amityville 1992,* and *The Tie That Binds.* He has made guest-star appearances on *The Pretender, Party of Five, Reasonable Doubts, The Wonder Years, Sisters, Crime Story,* and *Thirtysomething.* Bourland has appeared in countless TV commercials and has made the transition into commercial directing.

Maria Canals

Maria Canals' feature films credits are *Imagining Argentina, The Master of Disguise, America's Sweethearts, Dawg, My Family/Mi Familia,* and *Cop and a Half.* On television, Canals has been a series regular on *The Tony Danza Show, Freddy Soto* (pilot), *Harlan & Merleen, Marielena,* and *Corte Tropical.* She has been a recurring character on *Curb Your Enthusiasm, Brothers Garcia, American Family, Beggars and Choosers, Culture Clash,* and *Key West.* Canals was nominated for an Ovation Award for *Changes of Heart* at the

Mark Taper Forum and is the recipient of a 2002 Alma Award for best supporting actress.

Nestor Carbonell

Nestor Carbonell has been a series regular on *Century City, The Tick*, and *Suddenly Susan*. His guest-star appearances include *Scrubs, Monk, Ally McBeal*, and a recurring role on *Resurrection Blvd*. On film he has been featured in *The Lost City, Manhood, The Laramie Project, Jack the Dog, Noriega, Attention Shoppers* (writer credit), and *New Suits*. On stage he has performed at the Old Globe Theater, American Repertory Theater, and Harvard University.

Willie C. Carpenter

Willie C. Carpenter appeared on Broadway in *Musical Comedy Murders–1940*, and regionally at the Paper Mill Playhouse and the Pasadena Playhouse. His theater credits include the Signature Theater, Theater Geo, Rose Theater, Doolittle Theater, Mark Taper Forum, and the NYSF. Films credits are *The Underground, Hunter's Moon, The Insider, The Best Man, Men in Black, White Man's Burden, Mi Familia, Hard Target, Little Giants*, and *Amityville V*. Carpenter has made numerous guest-star appearances on such shows as *Cosby, Chicago Hope, Ellen, The Big House, Gilmore Girls, The District, Third Watch*, and *The Client*. He is the recipient of a Drama-Logue Award for *Up the Mountain* and an NAACP Award for best supporting actor in *Mr. Rickey Calls a Meeting*.

Michael Paul Chan trained at the American Conservatory Theater and performed on such stages as the New York Shakespeare Festival, the Mark Taper Forum, the Milwaukee Rep, and the East West Players. He was a founding member of the Asian-American Players. A partial list of his

Michael Paul Chan

thirty film credits includes *Mrs. Harris, Spy Game, The Insider, Once in the Life, The Joy Luck Club, Batman and Robin, Batman Forever, Heaven and Earth, Maverick, Falling Down,* and *Thousand Pieces of Gold.* He was a series regular on *Robbery Homicide Division* and *The PJs* and has had countless guest appearances on such shows as *Las Vegas, Boomtown, JAG, Arrested Development, Crossing Jordan, VIP, Nikki,* and *The Wonder Years.* Chan is the voice of Jimmy Ho on *The PJs.*

John P. Connolly

John P. Connolly is the current president of AFTRA (American Federation of Television and Radio Artists). His Broadway credits include *Big River* and *Company.* In New York he has appeared on stage at the American Place Theater, Manhattan Theater Club, NYSF, and Playhouse 91. In Los Angeles he has performed at the Mark Taper Forum, Odyssey Theatre, and the Pasadena Playhouse. Regionally he's performed at Syracuse Stage, Hartman Theater, Walnut, Milwaukee Rep, and Cincinnati Playhouse. He has been a television series regular on *Sessions, Laurel Canyon,* and *Crash* and played a recurring character on *West Wing, Family Law,* and *General Hospital.* Movie of the week credits include *Toothless, Innocent Victims, Confessions, Internal Affairs, Kojak, Midnight Run, Murder,* and *Memory.* Film credits include *Je'Mappelle Crawford, When the Bough Breaks, 9½ Weeks, Hard Choices, King of Prussia,* and *Silver Bullet.*

Anne DeSalvo appeared on Broadway in *Gemini* and *Safe Sex.* She performed on Off Broadway in *The Nature and Purpose of the Universe, The Transfiguration of Benno Blimpie,* and *The Sorrows of Stephen,* to name but a few. She also sang in *Godbless You, Mr. Rosewater* and *Girls, Girls, Girls* at the Public Theater. She won a best actress award for her performance in *Lend*

Anne DeSalvo

Me a Tenor at the Pasadena Playhouse. DeSalvo has starred in such films as *Stardust Memories, Arthur, My Favorite Year, Perfect, Compromising Positions, Burglar*, and *Taking Care of Business*. Movies of the week include *Dead in the Water, The Last Tenant* with Lee Strasberg, and *Almost a Woman*. She was a series regular on *Man in the Family* and has had countless TV guest-star appearances. DeSalvo is the writer-director of two critically acclaimed award-winning independent films: *Women Without Implants* and *The Amati Girls*.

Nike Doukas

Nike Doukas has worked extensively on stage at such theaters as South Coast Repertory, the Old Globe, Berkeley Repertory, American Conservatory Theater, A Contemporary Theater, Berkeley Shakespeare Festival, the Doolittle, Pasadena Playhouse, and the Mark Taper Forum. Some of her roles include Barbara in *Major Barbara*, Beatrice in *Much Ado About Nothing*, Sonya in *The Wood Demon*, Portia in *Julius Caesar*, Sybil in *Private Lives*, Mrs. Webb in *Our Town*, Lady Anne in *Richard III*, and Desdemona in *Othello*. Nike has made guest appearances on *NYPD 2069, The Guardian, NYPD Blue, Malcom in the Middle, Judging Amy, ER*, and *Almost Perfect*. She was featured on film in *Seven Girlfriends and '68*. Doukas graduated with an MFA from the American Conservatory Theatre.

Christine Estabrook is a graduate of the Yale Drama School and has appeared on Broadway in *The Sisters Rosensweig, The Heidi Chronicles, I'm Not Rappaport, The Inspector General*, and *The Cherry Orchard*. She is the recipient of two Drama Desk Awards for her work in *The Boys*

Christine Estabrook

Next Door and *North Shore Fish*. She has been a series regular on *The Crew, Hometown, Road Hogs, The Nikki Cox Show, The Secret Diary of Desmond Pfeiffer,* and *My Wonderful Life* and a recurring character on *Desperate Housewives*. Movie of the week roles include *Murder Live, Journey to Mars, One Special Victory, Hometown,* and *The Wall*. On film she has been seen in *Spider-Man-2, Desperate Measures, Usual Suspects, Sea of Love, Second Sight,* and *Almost You*.

Richard Fancy

Richard Fancy has appeared on Broadway in *Singin' in the Rain* and Off Broadway in *Kind Lady* and *Rites of Passage*. His many film credits include *Shopgirl, Untitled Onion Movie, The Girl Next Door, Moonlight Mile, Psycho Beach Party, Being John Malkovich, Eat Your Heart Out, Touch, Nixon, Species, Till There Was You, Tango and Cash, Identity Crisis,* and *Richie Rich's Christmas Wish*. On television he has had recurring roles on *The District, Girls Club, Third Rock from the Sun, Seinfeld, Diagnosis Murder, Orleans, LA Law,* and *Doogie Howser* as well as countless guest-star appearances. Movie of the week roles include *Primal Force, Innocent Victim, Untamed Love, Roswell, And the Band Played On,* and *Drive Like Lightning*. Fancy is a member of the Pacific Resident Theater.

Ashley Gardner has appeared on Broadway in *Hay Fever* and with Circle Repertory, Stage Three, and the York Theater in New York. Regionally she has performed with Delaware Theater Company, the McCarter Theater, Peterborough Players, and NCSA Actors Ensemble. Her film

Ashley Gardner

credits include *Johnny Suede, He Said, She Said, Heart of Dixie*, and *Kaos on Warwick Avenue*. She has a recurring voice role on *King of the Hill*. Gardner has been a recurring guest star on *Madman of the People, Grace Under Fire, Drew Carey*, and *Michael Hayes*. A selected list of television appearances includes *Strong Medicine, ER, Six Feet Under, Ellen, Charmed, Spin City, Just Shoot Me, Judging Amy, Becker*, and the TV movie *Complex of Fear*.

Lee Garlington

Lee Garlington has appeared in more than thirty motion pictures including *A Lot Like Love, American Pie 2, Lovely and Amazing, One Hour Photo, Evolution, Dante's Peak, My Life, Sneakers, Field of Dreams*, and *Psycho II and III*. Her score of credits for movies of the week and miniseries include *The Detective, If These Walls Could Talk II, Prodigal Son, Virtual Obsession, Summer of Fear, Cold Sassy Tree*, and *Shame*. Her numerous television credits include nine pilots and series regular work on *Arresting Behavior, Flying Colors*, and *Townies*. She's had recurring episodic appearances on *Judging Amy, Grace Under Fire, Roseanne, Abby Newton*, and *Everwood* as well as countless guest-star roles. Garlington received an Ovation Award for her stage work in *Risk Everything* and has been on stage at the Pasadena Playhouse and Hudson, Odyssey, and Powerhouse Theaters.

Mary Pat Gleason

Mary Pat Gleason has appeared in more than twenty motion pictures including *Traffic, The Crucible, Lorenzo's Oil, Basic Instinct, Man Trouble, Defending Your Life, Soapdish, Troop Beverly Hills, This Ain't Beebop*, and *Fat Man and Little Boy*. She has guest starred in more than fifty episodic television shows as varied as *Will and Grace, NYPD Blue, ER, Murphy Brown, Coach, Who's the Boss, Life Goes On*, and *Friends*. Her movie of the week credits include *A Season for Miracles, Right to Remain Silent*, and *The Story Lady*. She has won an Emmy for writing for the soap opera *Guiding Light* and has appeared on *General Hospital* and *Texas*. On stage she has performed at the Manhattan Theater Club, Pasadena Playhouse, and the Mark Taper Forum.

April Grace

April Grace has appeared in more than a dozen motion pictures, including *Constantine, A.I., Finding Forrester, Magnolia, Playing by Heart, Waterproof, Chicago Cab, Wolverton Mountain, Safe, The Beneficiary*, and *Angie, I Says*. She's been a series regular on *Medium* and *The Beast* and had recurring guest-star work on *Joan of Arcadia, Strong Medicine, The Shield, The O.C., Chicago Hope*, and *Boston Public*. Grace received Drama-Logue Awards for her work in *Spunk* at San Diego Repertory and *The Rabbit Foot* at Los Angeles Theatre Center. She has also appeared on stage at the Mark Taper Forum, Tamarind Theater, East Coast Arts, and Mumbo Jumbo Theater Company.

H. Richard Greene

H. Richard Greene was a resident member of the Repertory Theatre of Lincoln Center, appearing in *Mary Stuart, Twelfth Night, Narrow Road to the Deep North, Play Strindberg,* and *The Crucible.* His other Broadway credits include *The Survivor, Romeo and Juliet,* and *Brighton Beach Memoirs.* On Off Broadway, he originated the role of Bobby Stein in *Family Business* and for PBS' American Playhouse. Regional credits include Yale Repertory Theatre, Williamstown Theatre, Buffalo Studio Arena, and the Old Globe San Diego. He has recurring roles on *The West Wing* and *Boston Legal* and has had appearances on *The District, The Practice, NYPD Blue,* and *Without a Trace.*

Luck Hari

Luck Hari has appeared as Anya in the *Cherry Orchard* and Eliante in *The Misthanthrope* at South Coast Repertory. She performed the role of Helena in *All's Well That Ends Well* and Iras in *Anthony and Cleopatra* for the Oregon Shakespeare Festival. At Shakespeare Santa Cruz she has played Emily in *Our Town* and Olivia in *Twelfth Night.* On television Hari was a recurring character for four years on *Frasier* and had recurring roles on *Girlfriends, ER, Providence, The Bernie Mac Show,* and *Presidio Med.* Her television movie credits are *The Princess and the Marine* and *Baby Brokers.* Guest-starring roles include *NYPD, Everybody Loves Raymond, The District, Six Feet Under, Ally McBeal,* and *Chicago Hope.*

Magda Harout

Magda Harout has performed on stage at the Pasadena Playhouse, the Mark Taper Forum, and Tiffany Theatre in Los Angeles. She has won acting awards from *LA Weekly*, Drama-Logue, and LA Drama Critics Circle. Harout has appeared in *General Hospital*, *The Young and the Restless*, *Days of Our Lives*, and *Santa Barbara*. Some of her many guest appearances include *The Practice*, *The Agency*, *Without a Trace*, *Tracey Takes On*, *Seinfeld*, *Newhart*, and *The Nanny*. Her film credits include *Song of the Lark*, *Pro Bono*, *Size' Em Up*, *9½ Ninjas*, and *My Life*.

Roxanne Hart

Roxanne Hart has appeared on Broadway in *Equus*, *Loose Ends*, *Passion*, *Cheaters*, and *The Devil's Disciple*. For her stage work, Hart has been nominated for a Tony Award and is a recipient of a Drama-Logue and a Theatre World Award. On television she has been a series regular on *Chicago Hope* and had guest appearances on *The Agency*, *Family Law*, *Law & Order*, and *ER*. TV movie credits are *The Runaway*, *Follow the Stars Home*, *Come On–Get Happy*, *Alone*, *Meteorite*, *Big Time*, *Special Bulletin*, *Samaritan*, and *Kent State*. Her film credits include *Moonlight Mile*, *Good Girl*, *Homeroom*, *Once Around*, *The Highlander*, *Old Enough*, *Oh God! You Devil*, and *The Verdict*.

Barry Shabaka Henley

Barry Shabaka Henley has appeared in more than twenty motion pictures, including *Collateral, The Terminal, Pavement, Ali, Go with the Fro, Patch Adams, How Stella Got Her Groove Back, Bulworth,* and *Devil in a Blue Dress.* He has been a series regular on *Robbery Homicide Division* and *Gang, Die.* His notable TV guest appearances include *Law & Order: SVU, Providence, Crossing Jordan, Brooklyn South, Johnny Bago,* and *Oz.* Henley is a member of the San Fransisco Mime Troupe and has acted extensively at Los Angeles Theater Company (LATC).

Amy Hill

Amy Hill is the recipient of a Drama-Logue Award for creating and performing her solo piece *Reunion.* She has also appeared on stage at Lincoln Center, Berkeley Repertory, NYSF, and Ensemble Studio Theater. Film credits include *Unbeatable Harold, Kids in America, Duck, Cheaper by the Dozen, 50 First Dates, Dr. Seuss' Cat in the Hat, Big Fat Liar, Rising Sun, Dim Sum,* and *Living on Tokyo Time.* Amy has been a series regular on *All American Girl, Maybe This Time, Pauly, Jon Lovitz* (pilot), and *Strip Mall.* Some of her many guest-star appearances are *Six Feet Under, Reno 911, Frasier, Bernie Mac, Curb Your Enthusiasm, Friends,* and *The Proud Family* (voice).

Rif Hutton

Rif Hutton's partial list of film credits includes *Restraining Order, Big Foot, Going Under, Stand and Deliver, Shotgun Jones, Hollywood Homicide, The Thirteenth Floor, Quality Time, Star Trek: Generations, Death Becomes Her, Moving,* and *The Force.* Hutton has had recurring guest appearances on *JAG, Getting By, Doogie Howser, M.D., The Bold and the Beautiful, General Hospital,* and *The Young and the Restless.* Some of his numerous guest-star appearances have been on *The Shield, Cold Case, Monk, Century City, CSI: Miami, Buffy, Home Improvement,* and *Sister, Sister.* He has appeared on stage at the L.A. Shakespeare Festival, Will Geer Theatricum Botanicum, Laguna Beach Playhouse, and the Victoria Theater and Hippodrome in San Francisco.

Gregory Itzin

Gregory Itzin is the winner of the LA Drama Critics Award for his stage work at the Matrix Theatre for *The Homecoming* and *Waiting for Godot.* He was nominated for a Tony and a Drama Desk Award for his work in *The Kentucky Cycle.* His film credits include *Adaptation, Original Sin, Dad, Fear and Loathing in Las Vegas,* and *The Fabulous Baker Boys.* He has appeared as a television series regular on *24, Murder One, Strip Mall,* and *Something Wilder* and as a recurring character on *The Practice, Profiler, JAG, Beggars and Choosers, Judging Amy, Philly,* and *Party of Five.*

Lucinda Jenney

Lucinda Jenney made her Broadway debut in *Gemini*. She appeared on stage at the Long Wharf Theatre in *Tobacco Road* and *Dalliance*, at the Williamstown Theatre Festival in *Miss Julie*, and Off Broadway in *Rosemary with Ginger* and *Aven'U Boys*. A partial list of film credits include *S.W.A.T*, *Mothman Prophecies*, *Thirteen Days*, *Sugar Town*, *Mad City*, *G.I. Jane*, *Grace of My Heart*, *American Heart* (Spirit Award nomination), *Thelma & Louise*, *Rain Man*, *Peggy Sue Got Married*, and *Wired*. She was a series regular on *The Shield* and had a recurring role on *24*. Guest-star appearances include *House*, *Six Feet Under*, *Law & Order*, *The West Wing*, *Carnivale*, *Judging Amy*, *The Practice*, *NYPD Blue*, and *Homicide*.

Brent Jennings

Brent Jennings' film credits include *Witness*, *A Lesson Before Dying*, *Boycott*, *Brubaker*, *Red Heat*, *Kansas*, *Life*, *The Serpent and the Rainbow*, and *Another 48 Hours*. He has been a series regular on *Hopewell* and *The Antagonist* and had recurring roles on *ER* and *Brooklyn Bridge*. Broadway credits include *G.R. Point* and *The Mighty Gents*. He's performed on Off Broadway at the New York Shakespeare Festival, Phoenix Theatre, Manhattan Theater Club, and American Place Theater. Movie of the week credits are *Boycott*, *A Lesson Before Dying*, *The Fixer*, *Don King*, *Love Songs*, *Soul of the Game*, *George McKenna Story*, *Child's Cry*, *Pointman*, and *In the Line of Duty*.

Juanita Jennings

Juanita Jennings won a 1994 Cable Ace Award as best supporting actress for her work on HBO's *Laurel Avenue*. She has had a recurring part on *The Division* and *City of Angels* and had countless guest-starring roles on such episodic television shows as *The Practice, Judging Amy, The Pretender, Felicity,* and *7th Heaven*. Her film credits include *Runaway Jury, Spirit Lost, Color of Night, Basic Instinct, Love Child, Baby Boy, Dancing in September,* and *What Women Want*. On stage she toured in the national production of *Home* and performed at the Negro Ensemble Company, Richard Allen Center, Women's Inter Art, LATC, the Old Globe, and Mark Taper Forum. She is a recipient of a 1995 NAACP Award for her work in *Jar the Floor* at South Coast Repertory Theatre.

Anne-Marie Johnson

Anne-Marie Johnson has appeared on film in *Down in the Delta, Strictly Business, Hollywood Shuffle, Robot Jox, Five Hearbeats,* and *I'm Gonna Git U Sucka*. She has been a TV series regular on *Double Trouble, What's Happening Now, In the Heat of the Night, In Living Color, Melrose Place, Smart Guy* (pilot), *Manhattan Man* (pilot), and *Guy Island* (pilot). Johnson has been a recurring character on *Girlfriends, Abby,* and *JAG* and has made guest-star appearances on *The Parkers, Strong Medicine, The X-Files, The District, Ally McBeal,* and *Chicago Hope*. TV films are *Lucky Chances* and *Asteroids*.

Eddie Jones

Eddie Jones has appeared in more than a dozen films, including *Seabiscuit, Prince of the City, The Grifters, Sneakers, Cadillac Man, The Rocketeer, Stanley and Iris,* and *A League of Their Own.* He has been a series regular on *Lois and Clark* and *Invisible Man.* His many recurring television credits include *EZ Streets, Grand, The Equalizer,* and *Dark Shadows.* Movie of the week roles include *Pro Bono, The Day Lincoln Was Shot, The Fitzgeralds and Kennedys, Texas Cheerleader-Murdering Mom, Switch,* and *Final Appeal.* Broadway credits include *That Championship Season, Devour the Snow,* and work at Manhattan Theater Club, Hudson Guild, and Vineyard Theater. In Los Angeles he portrayed Willie Loman in *Death of a Salesman* at the Interact Theatre.

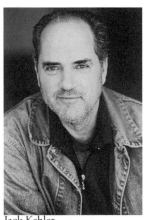

Jack Kehler

Jack Kehler has been featured in more than thirty motion pictures, including *Men in Black II, The Big Lebowski, Forces of Nature, Waterworld, Wyatt Earp, 187, The Last Boy Scout, Under the Tuscan Sun, Year of the Dragon, Lesser Evil, Austin Powers,* and *True Crime.* Kehler was a series regular on *McKenna* and some of his guest-star roles have been on *The Practice, NYPD Blue, ER, 7th Heaven, Ellen, Newhart, Hill Street Blues, Beggars and Choosers,* and *Wings.* His movie of the week credits include *Texas Cheer-leader-Murdering Mom* and *If These Walls Could Talk.* Kehler is a member of the Actors Studio.

Sheila Kelley

Sheila Kelley was a television series regular on *LA Law, Moving Story*, and *Sisters* as well as a recurring character on *ER* and *MDs*. Her television movies include *Tonight's the Night, The Betty Ford Story, The Chase, Deconstructing Sarah, The Secretary*, and *The Jennie Project*. Her motion picture credits include *Singles, Dancing at the Blue Iguana, The Secretary, Mona Must Die, Rules of Obsession, One Fine Day*, and *Nurse Betty*. She played the role of Blanche DuBois in the American Conservatory Theatre Production of *A Streetcar Named Desire*. Kelley is the author of *The S Factor*.

Shannon Kenny

Shannon Kenny has been a series regular on *Invisible Man, Taking Liberty, Muscle*, and *Sons and Daughters*. She has had recurring roles on *7th Heaven* and *Savannah* and guest-star appearances on *The Guardian, The Naked Truth, Seinfeld, Ned* and *Stacey*, and *Almost Perfect*. Her motion picture credits include *The Big K, The Visitor, Timemaster, Bodily Harm*, and *Give Way When Merging*. She has performed on stage at San Jose Repertory and Shakespeare Santa Cruz and is a graduate of the California Institute of the Arts.

Emily Kuroda

Emily Kuroda has completed her fourth year on *Gilmore Girls*. Other TV credits include *Six Feet Under, The Practice, King of Queens, ER, The Division, Curb Your Enthusiasm, The Agency,* and *Arliss*. Feature film credits are *Minority Report, Stranger Inside, Two Days in the Valley, DAD, Broken Words, About Love* (Emmy nomination), *Worth Winning,* and *Shop Girl*. Emily is the recipient of five Drama-Logue Awards, a Garland, and an LA Ovation nomination for her stage work. Emily has performed in more than thirty-five productions for the East West Players in Los Angeles. Other stage appearances are South Coast Rep, NYSF, La Jolla Playhouse, Seattle Rep, Singapore Repertory Theater, Doolittle Theater, and Huntington Theater.

Clyde Kusatsu

Clyde Kusatsu has appeared in more than sixty motion pictures, movies of the week, and miniseries. A partial list of credits include *Extreme Dating, Hollywood Homicide, The United States of Leland, American Pie, Godzilla, Dragon: The Bruce Lee Story, Hot Shots: Part Deux, In the Line of Fire, American Tragedy, Wired, Mistress, Turner and Hooch,* and *Shanghai Surprise*. His more than one hundred TV guest appearances include *Providence, Nip/Tuck, Family Law, Citizen Baines, JAG, Malcom in the Middle, Ally McBeal, The West Wing, Dharma & Greg, Star Trek: TNG,* and *Magnum, P.I.* As a voice-over artist, he can be heard in *House of Mouse, Mickey Mouse Works, Jem, Where on Earth Is Carmen Sandiego?* and many more. He is a graduate of the theater school at Northwestern University.

Hal Landon

Hal Landon is a founding member of South Coast Repertory Theater. A partial list of his major roles are Orgon in *Tartuffe*, Vladimir in *Waiting for Godot*, Teach in *American Buffalo*, Bradley in *Buried Child*, Scrooge in *A Christmas Carol*, Joe in *Time of Your Life*, Prospero in *The Tempest*, Astrov in *Uncle Vanya*, and Williamson in *Glengarry Glen Ross*. On film Landon has appeared in *Bill and Ted's Excellent Adventure, Bogus Journey, The Breakup, Speakeasy, Little Death, Trespass, Eraserhead, Pacific Heights, Prison*, and *Playing by Heart*. He's been a series regular on *Muddling Through* and had guest appearances on *Frasier, Ellen, Star Trek: Deep Space Nine, Murphy Brown, Matlock*, and *Newhart*. His TV movie credits are *Life of the Party, Every Knee Shall Bow*, and *Sunset Limousine*.

Marcella Lowery

Marcella Lowery has performed on Broadway in *Lolita* and *Member of the Wedding*. Her Off-Broadway credits include *Your Obituary Is a Dance, Before It Hits Home, Sugar Hill, Ladies, Baseball Wives*, and *Jamimma*. Marcella was a series regular on *City Guys* and *Ghostwriter* and had appearances on *The Cosby Show, New York News, Hawk, Monsters, Law & Order*, and many other shows. On film she has been featured in *The Preacher's Wife, Nine Months, What About Bob, New Jack City, Lean on Me, Arthur, Fletch II*, and *Kramer vs. Kramer*. Lowery has acted in countless television commercials.

Aaron Lustig

Aaron Lustig has appeared in twenty motion pictures including *Bedazzled, Space Cowboys, Darkman, Gun Shy, Stuart Saves the Family, Ghostbusters II,* and *Edward Scissorhands.* Aaron was nominated for an Emmy for his acting work on *The Young and the Restless.* His extensive television credits include recurring work on *Family Law, NYPD Blue, Tracey Takes On,* and *Party of Five.* Movie of the week credits include *The Late Shift, If These Walls Could Talk, Gilligan's Island,* and *A Mother's Prayer.* His voice has been heard in the animated series *Rugrats, The Family Guy, The Wild Thornberrys,* and *Duckman.* Lustig has acted on stage at St. Clements, Soho Rep, Barter Theater, and the New Jersey Shakespeare Festival.

Julio Oscar Mechoso

Julio Oscar Mechoso's list of more than thirty motion picture roles includes *Lords of Dogtown, Lost City, Once Upon a Time in Mexico, Jurassic Park III, Bad Boys, All the Pretty Horses, Phone Booth, Mad City, Blue Streak, White Squall, Toys,* and *Internal Affairs.* Mechoso has been a series regular on *Greetings from Tucson, Damon,* and *High Incident.* TV movie credits are *Back When We Were Young, Missing Pieces, Day of Reckoning, For Love or Country, Atticus, Deadly Games,* and *The Take.* Some of his many guest-star appearances include *Kingpin, NYPD Blue, Seinfeld, Murphy Brown, Coach,* and *Birdland.* He is also the artistic director and Founder of the Venice Beach Players.

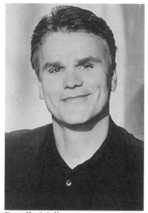

Randle Mell

Randle Mell was nominated for a Drama Desk Award in John Houseman's production of *The Cradle Will Rock*. His Broadway credits include *The Rainmaker, Macbeth,* and *Noises Off.* Randle has acted on stage at the Mark Taper Forum, La Jolla Playhouse, Arena Stage, and the Guthrie Theater. He has been a member of such notable repertory companies as the Actors Theatre of Louisville and the Acting Company. A partial list of his motion picture credits includes *Cookie's Fortune, Wyatt Earp, Eight Men Out, Postman, City of Hope, Grand Canyon,* and *Fearless.* Some of his guest appearances include *Law & Order, Nash Bridges, Kingpin, The Client,* and *24.* Movie of the week work includes *O Pioneers, The Cradle Will Rock, Kennedys of Massachusetts, A Few Good Hearts, A Mother's Gift,* and *Separate but Equal.*

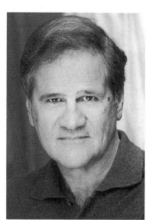

Stephen Mendillo

Stephen Mendillo, a graduate of the Yale Drama School, has appeared on Broadway in such diverse plays as *Guys and Dolls, Orpheus Descending, Our Town, A View from the Bridge,* and *Ah, Wilderness.* His extensive Off-Broadway credits include work at the New York Shakespeare Festival, Playwrights Horizon, Manhattan Theatre Club, Circle Repertory, and the WPA Theatre (an Off-Broadway theater company). Some of his dozen films are *G.I. Jane, Eight Men Out, Slapshot, Cobb, Lianna, City of Hope,* and *Broadcast News.* He has been a TV series regular in *Parole, Today FBI,* and *Key West* and had numerous guest-star appearances on *Alias, Law & Order, The Equalizer,* and *Soap.*

Debra Monk

Debra Monk is a recipient of a Tony Award for her performance in *Redwood Curtain* and was twice nominated for her work in *Steel Pier* and *Picnic*. Other Broadway credits include *Thou Shalt Not, Ah, Wilderness, Company, Nick & Nora, Prelude to a Kiss,* and *Pumpboys and Dinettes,* which she also coauthored. She has won an Obie Award for *The Time of the Cuckoo* and a Drama Desk Award for *Oil City Symphony.* Monk won an Emmy for her recurring role on *NYPD Blue* as Katie Sipowicz. A partial list of her film credits includes *Briar Patch, Center Stage, Devil's Advocate, In and Out, Extreme Measures, First Wives Club, The Bridges of Madison County, Prelude to a Kiss, Substance of Fire, Fearless, Quiz Show, For Love or Money,* and *Jeffrey.* Monk holds an MFA from Southern Methodist University.

Shelley Morrison

Shelley Morrison has had a four-decade career as an actor. Her film credits include *Fools Rush In, Troop Beverly Hills, Max Dugan Returns, Blume in Love, The Greatest Story Ever Told, McKenna's Gold, Divorce American Style, Funny Girl,* and *Shark Tale.* She has been a series regular on *Will and Grace,* winning the SAG Best Ensemble Award for acting. Other television series appearances are *Courthouse, The Flying Nun,* several pilots, and recurring roles on *The Farmer's Daughter, Laredo,* and *General Hospital.* A partial list of guest-star appearances include *Prey, LA Law, Sisters, First and Ten, The Rookies, Marcus Welby, M.D., Dr. Kildare, The Fugitive, Playhouse 90,* and *My Favorite Martian.* Morrison has been nominated for an ALMA Award and is listed in *Who's Who of Hispanic Women.*

Marianne Muellerleile

Marianne Muellerleile has appeared in more than thirty-five motion pictures, including *Return to Me, Liar, Liar, The Road to Wellville, The Terminator, Mad City, Soap Dish, Heaven and Earth, Passion Fish, Life Stinks, Memento, Revenge of the Nerds, A Dangerous Woman, Jingle All the Way,* and *One Fine Day.* She's had more than 175 television guest appearances. She was a series regular on *Life with Bonnie* and had recurring roles on *Passions, 3rd Rock from the Sun, Saved by the Bell, Journey of Allen Strange,* and *The Young and The Restless.* She's had more than fifty stage appearances and has performed at Playwrights Horizons, Coconut Grove, New Dramatists, and Minnesota Opera Company.

Lupe Ontiveros

Lupe Ontiveros has appeared on stage in *Zoot Suit* in both Los Angeles and New York. A founding member of the Latino Theater Company in Los Angeles, she also acted at the San Diego Repertory Company, Borderland Theatre Tucson, and Los Angeles Theater Center. Her film credits include *Real Women Have Curves, Passionada, Adaptation, Storytelling, Chuck and Buck, As Good as It Gets, Selena, The Brave, Mi Familia, El Norte/The North,* and *Zoot Suit.* On television she has been a series regular on *The Adventures of Maya and Miguel, Greetings from Tucson,* and *Dudley* and had recurring roles on *Desperate Housewives, Pasadena, Brothers Garcia, Veronica's Closet,* and *I Married Dora.* She is the recipient of the Nostoros Golden Eagle Award, the Alma Award, the Special Jury at the Sundance Film Festival, a National Board of Review Award, and an Emmy nomination. She is the first Latina to win a Maverick Award.

Ethan Phillips

Ethan Phillips has appeared on and off Broadway in such shows as *My Favorite Year* at the Lincoln Center, *Lips Together Teeth Apart* at the Lucille Lortel, and *Modiglianni* at the Astor Place Theater. Other stage venues have been the New York Shakespeare Festival, Ensemble Studio Theater, Playwrights Horizons, Old Globe, Baltimore Center Stage, the Actors Theatre of Louisville, and Seattle Rep. In Los Angeles he has performed at the Mark Taper Forum, Coronet Theater, and the Pasadena Playhouse. Phillips is recognized for his television work as Neelix in *Star Trek: Voyager* and Pete in *Benson*. Film credits include *For Richer or Poorer*, *Star Trek: First Contact*, *Greencard*, *Man Without a Face*, *Jeffrey*, *Critters*, *The Shadow*, *Ragtime*, *Lean on Me*, and *Bad Santa*. Ethan has participated for ten years at the Sundance Institute and is the author of the play *Penguin Blues*.

Robert Picardo

Robert Picardo first appeared on Broadway in *Gemini*, followed by *Tribute*, with Jack Lemmon. His Los Angeles theater credits include *The Waiting Room*, *On the 20th Century* (Ovation Award nomination), and *A Class Act* at the Pasadena Playhouse. Picardo was a series regular on *Star Trek: Voyager* and *China Beach* and was nominated for an Emmy for his recurring work on *The Wonder Years*. Some of his many guest appearances are *West Wing*, *The Lyon's Den*, *The Practice*, *ER*, *Stargate SG-1*, and *LA Law*. A partial list of his more than twenty film credits include *Looney Tunes: Back in Action*, *Amati Girls*, *Star Trek: First Contact*, *Gremlins II*, *976-Evil*, *The Howling*, *Star 80*, *Explorers*, *Wagons East*, and *Total Recall*.

Vic Polizos

Vic Polizos has appeared in more than twenty-five motion pictures, including *Harlem Nights, Prizzi's Honor, Winchell, 187, Flesh and Bone, Russkies, Falcon and the Snowman, Brubaker, Peter Gunn,* and *The Muppets Take Manhattan.* He has appeared on Broadway and on stages throughout the country, including at the Eugene O'Neil Playwrights Conference and the Williamstown Theater Festival. Polizos has guest starred on numerous episodic television shows such as *Party of Five, The X-Files, Arliss, Grace Under Fire, NYPD Blue, Diagnosis Murder, The Pretender,* and *Seinfeld.*

Carol Potter

Carol Potter is a graduate of the Yale Drama School. Her Broadway credits include *Gemini* and *The Lady from Dubuque.* Potter has appeared on stage at Ahmanson Theater in *Summer and Smoke,* Playwrights Horizons, Circle Rep, Equity Library Theater, and Williamstown Theater Festival. Potter created the character Cindy Walsh on *Beverly Hills, 90210.* In addition she was a series regular on *Today's FBI* and a contract player on *Sunset Beach.* Her guest-star appearances include *NYPD Blue, Providence, LA Law,* and *Highway to Heaven.* Her film credits are *Naturally Native, Tigerheart,* and *Dutch Treat.*

Barry Primus

Barry Primus is a member of the Actors Studio and the famed Lincoln Center Repertory with Elia Kazan. On stage he has worked at the New York Shakespeare Festival, Yale Repertory, Arena Theater, and Theater Company of Boston. His more than thirty film appearances include *Life Is a House, New York, New York, The Rose, Absence of Malice, Forbidden Love, Loon, The River, Boxcar Bertha, The Brotherhood, Deadly, Night and the City,* and *Down and Out in Beverly Hills.* He is the writer-director of the independent film *The Mistress.* On Broadway he appeared in *The Changeling, Creation of the World and Other Business, The Nervous Set,* and *Tible and Her Denson.* Movie of the week credits include *James Dean Story, Crime of the Century, Daytona Blues, Trade Off, Brotherly Love,* and *Shut Down.* He was also a series regular on *Cagney and Lacey.*

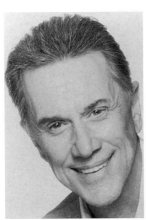

Andrew Prine

Andrew Prine made his Broadway debut in the Pulitzer Prize–winning play *Look Homeward, Angel.* Other notable stage appearances include *A Distant Bell* on Broadway and *Long Day's Journey into Night, The Caine Mutiny,* and *Mr. Roberts* at the Ahmanson Theater in Los Angeles. Prine is the recipient of two Drama-Logue Awards for *Freddy's Dead* and *Buried Child* and an *LA Weekly* Theater Award for *They Shoot Horses, Don't They?* Some of his many film credits are *The Miracle Worker, Gettysburg, The Avenging Angel, Chisum, The Devil's Brigade, Amityville, Riding Tall, Possums,* and *James Dean.* He's been a series regular on *Wide Country, The Road West, W.E.B., Room for Two,* and *V* and had countless guest-star appearances on episodic television. Prine hosts *Conversations* for the Western Channel and has a recurring role on *Six Feet Under.* He is a member of the Actors Studio.

James Rebhorn

James Rebhorn has appeared on stage at the Vivian Beaumont in *Dinner at Eight, The Man Who Had All the Luck* for the Williamstown Theater Festival, *Far East* and *A Blooming of Ivy* at Lincoln Center, and *Twelve Angry Men* and *Our Town* on Broadway. His extensive theater credits include work at the NYSF, Ensemble Studio Theater (member), La Jolla Playhouse, and the Manhattan Theater Club. A partial list his of more than thirty film credits includes *Head of State, Scotland, Snow Falling on Cedars, Independence Day, Basic Instinct, Meet the Parents, Providence, The Talented Mr. Ripley, The Game, Carlito's Way, My Cousin Vinny,* and *Scent of a Woman.* Rebhorn has made numerous guest-star appearances on such shows as *Hack, Third Watch, Law & Order, Seinfeld, Kate and Allie, From Earth to the Moon, Reversible Errors,* and *Sarah Plain and Tall I* and *II.*

Lisa Blake Richards

Lisa Blake Richards is an accomplished stage actor who appeared on Broadway in the revival of *Sweet Bird of Youth* as well as in *Mourning Becomes Electra, Jumpers,* and *Love Suicide at Scholfield Barracks.* Off-Broadway credits include *Three Hotels, My Old Lady, Lay of the Land, Three Sisters, Marat/Sade,* and *Who's Afraid of Virginia Woolf?* She won a Drama-Logue Award for her role as Arcadina in *The Seagull.* On television Richards has been a contract player on *One Life to Live, Where the Heart Is,* and *Dark Shadows.* Her movie of the week credits are *Seasons of the Heart, David, Right to Kill, Who Will Love My Children?, Atlanta Child Murders,* and *City of Fear.* Her film credits include *Rolling Thunder, Mr. Mom, Heaven Can Wait, Eating, The Return, Verne Miller, House of Dark Shadows,* and *The Man Who Loved Women.* She is a member of the Actors Studio.

John Rothman

John Rothman has appeared on Broadway in *Social Security* and at the Vivian Beaumont Theatre in *Some Americans Abroad*. Off Broadway Rothman has worked at Playwrights Horizons, Variety Arts, the New Group, and regionally at the Long Wharf, Westport, Yale Rep, and the Berkshire Festival. He is a member of the Actors Studio and Ensemble Studio Theater and holds an MFA in acting from Yale University. Some of his many film credits include *Ghostbusters*, *Stardust Memories*, *The Purple Rose of Cairo*, *Zelig*, *Gettysburg*, *Pollack*, *Devil's Advocate*, *Big*, *The Ringer*, *Taxi*, *Daredevil*, and *Welcome to Mooseport*. He was a series regular on *Golden Years* and *Birdland* and had guest appearances on *Law & Order*, *Feds*, *NYPD Blue*, *Tales from the Darkside*, *100 Centre Street*, and the miniseries *Separate but Equal*.

Miguel Sandoval

Miguel Sandoval has appeared in more than thirty motion pictures, including *Clear and Present Danger*, *Get Shorty*, *Jurassic Park*, *The Crew*, *Jungle Fever*, *Collateral Damage*, *Human Nature*, *Blow*, *Panic*, *Route 9*, *Mrs. Winterbourne*, *Death Wish 5*, *Howard the Duck*, *Sid and Nancy*, and *Repo Man*. His more than thirty television movie credits include *For Love or Country: The Arturo Sandoval Story*, *TEXAS*, *La Pastorela*, *Confessions*, *The Fixer*, *Black Iris*, *Red Wind*, *Dangerous Dancing*, *Ned Blessing*, *The Cisco Kid*, *She Said No*, and *La Carpa*. He was a series regular on *The Court*, and *Fire Co. 132* and recurred on *Alias*, *7th Heaven*, *The Marshall*, *Seinfeld*, and *Murder One*. He is currently a series regular on *Medium*.

Klea Scott

Klea Scott has been a TV series regular on *Robbery Homicide Division, Metropolis, Millennium,* and *Brooklyn South.* Her guest-star appearances include *ER, Cosby, Just Shoot Me, Century City,* and the movie of the week *Sally Hemmings: An American Scandal.* Film credits include *Collateral, Minority Report,* and *Temptation.* She has appeared on stage at the New York Shakespeare Festival, the La Jolla Playhouse, the Mark Taper Forum, and Maui Onstage. Scott is a graduate of the North Carolina School of the Arts.

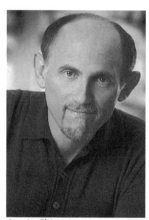

Armin Shimerman

Armin Shimerman has appeared on Broadway in *I Remember Mama, Broadway, St. Joan,* and *Three Penny Opera.* Regional credits include Mark Taper Forum, Tyrone Guthrie Theater, LATC, and San Diego Old Globe. He has been a series regular on *Star Trek: Deep Space Nine* and has had recurring work on *The Handler, Girls Club, For the People, Invisible Man, Buffy the Vampire Slayer, The Practice,* and *Brooklyn Bridge.* Shimerman has appeared in such films as *Stardust Memories, Blind Date, The Hitcher, Like Father Like Son, Dangerous Curves, Arena, Death Warrant,* and *Star Trek: Insurrection.* He received a best actor nomination for *Birthday Party* at the Matrix and is a recipient of a best supporting actor award in a comedy short for *Who Slew Simon Thaddeus Mulberry Pew?*

Lauren Tom

Lauren Tom has appeared on Broadway in *Hurlyburly, A Chorus Line,* and *Doonesbury.* She has performed at the NYSF, La Jolla Playhouse, Goodman Theater, and Vienna Festival. Some of her many film credits include *Bad Santa, City of Angels, Catfish in Black Bean Sauce, Joy Luck Club, Dear God, North, Mr. Jones,* and *Cadillac Man.* Tom has been a series regular on *DAG, Grace Under Fire, Cherry Street,* and *Culture Clash.* She has recurred on *The Division, Friends,* and *Homicide* and had guest appearances on *Thirtysomething, Anything but Love, Early Edition,* and *My Wife and Kids.* Tom is a recipient of a 1988 Obie Award for *American Notes* and two Drama-Logue Awards for *Tiger on the Right.*

Steve Vinovich

Steve Vinovich has appeared on Broadway in *Lost in Yonkers, The Secret Rapture, Loose Ends, The Robber Bridegroom, The Grand Tour,* and *The Magic Show.* Other stage work includes Paper Mill, Laguna and Pasadena Playhouses, Odyssey and Long Beach, Theaters, and the New York Shakespeare Festival. His feature film credits include *Rocket's Red Glare, Across the Line, Seven Girlfriends, I'll Do Anything, Mannequin, The Santa Clause,* and *Awakenings.* He was a series regular on *Going Places* and *Raising Miranda* and had recurring work on *The Hogan Family, Family Matters, Dilbert,* and *ER.* A partial list of guest-star appearances includes *Everybody Loves Raymond, JAG, Touched by an Angel, Ally McBeal, The Hughleys,* and *Chicago Hope.*

Recommended Reading

Belli, Mary Lou, and Phil Ramuno. 2004. *The Sitcom Career Book: A Guide to the Louder, Faster, Funnier World of TV Comedy.* New York: Backstage Books.

Bolles, Richard N. 2004. *What Color Is Your Parachute? A Practical Guide for Job Hunters and Career-Changers.* Berkeley, CA: Ten Speed.

Cameron, Julia, with Mark Bryan. 1992. *The Artist's Way.* New York: G. P. Putnam's Sons.

Campbell, Joseph, with Bill Moyers. 1988. *The Power of Myth.* New York: Doubleday.

Chopra, Deepak. 1994. *The Seven Spiritual Laws of Success: A Practical Guide to the Fulfillment of Your Dreams.* San Rafael, CA: New World Library.

Clurman, Harold. 1975. *The Fervent Years: The Group Theatre and the Thirties.* New York: Da Capo.

Hackett, Jean. 1993. *The Actor's Chekhov: Nikos Psacharopoulos and the Company of the Williamstown Theatre Festival, on the Plays of Anton Chekhov.* Newbury, VT: Smith and Kraus.

Hagen, Uta. 1973. *Respect for Acting.* New York: Macmillan.

Kerr, Judy. 1993. *Acting Is Everything: An Actor's Guidebook for a Successful Career in Los Angeles.* Studio City, CA: September.

May, Rollo. 1975. *The Courage to Create.* New York: W. W. Norton.

Meisner, Sanford, and Dennis Longwell. 1987. *Sanford Meisner on Acting.* New York: Vintage.

Owens, Gary, and Jeff Lenburg. 2005. *How to Make a Million Dollars with Your Voice (or Lose Your Tonsils Trying).* New York: McGraw Hill.

Porter, Kay. 2003. *The Mental Athlete.* Champaign, IL: Human Kinetics.

Rainford, Nancy. 2002. *How to Agent Your Agent.* Hollywood: IFilm.

See, Joan. 1998. *Acting in Commercials: A Guide to Auditioning and Performing on Camera.* New York: Backstage.

Shakespeare, William. 1993. *William Shakespeare: The Complete Works.* New York: Gramercy.

Shurtleff, Michael. 1978. *Audition—Everything an Actor Needs to Know to Get the Part.* New York: Walker.

Silverberg, Larry. 1996. *The Actor's Guide to Qualified Acting Coaches: Los Angeles.* Lyme, NH: Smith and Kraus.

———. 1996. *The Actor's Guide to Qualified Acting Coaches: New York.* Lyme, NH: Smith and Kraus.

Vogler, Christopher. 1992. *The Writer's Journey: Mythic Structures for Storytellers and Screenwriters.* Studio City, CA: Michael Wiese.